Angelika Dorothea Albrecht

THE TRIUMPH OF SPIRIT

Anthroposophy's Goetheanum Attracts the World

With 37 images
Front cover layout: www.clarissajochum.de
First "Goetheanum" building, aerial view 1921 from the south (image section)
www.wikiwand.com/de/Goetheanum
Back cover layout: www.clarissajochum.de
Second "Goetheanum" building, aerial view 1953 from the west (image section)
www.wikiwand.com/de/Goetheanum#/Zweites_Goetheanum
© 2023 Angelika Dorothea Albrecht
ang.albrecht@arcor.de
Printing set: www.clarissajochum.de
Production and publishing: BoD - Books on Demand, Norderstedt, Germany
Translation into English: Angelika Dorothea Albrecht
ISBN 9783753494807
2nd English edition 2023

*In all places where the manifold directions of the practical life
are renewed and transformed in the sense of Anthroposophy,
it is really a question of the concrete practice of resurrection power.
Anthroposophy is a path which leads man as ego being
to his full self-realization on the basis of the resurrection powers.*

Rudolf Steiner (1861 -1925)

Contents

Goetheanum – phonetic transcription: **Gø: tɔ á nʊm**.
Upon the recommendation of the Viennese language scientist Julius Schröer, Rudolf Steiner was invited by the German lexicographer Joseph Kürschner to edit Goethe's natural scientific scripts with introductions and ongoing explanations at the "Goethe- und Schiller-Archiv" in Weimar. From 1890 till 1897 he was engaged in this voluminous work. To honour Johann Wolfgang von Goethe and his natural-spiritual understanding of the world, Rudolf Steiner named the Dornach building "Goetheanum".

CW – means Complete Works comprising in numbers the complete edition of Rudolf Steiner's work as assigned by the "Rudolf Steiner Archiv" in Dornach, Switzerland starting in 1956. SteinerBooks has started to issue the CW numbers in English. The project aims to publish the entire set, volume for volume, following the German GA (= Gesamtausgabe). In 2006 the first volume (CW 28) was published. It will be many years before this monumental task is complete. Actually the complete edition of Rudolf Steiner's works in German comprises 354 numbers with c. 3,700 transcripts of a total of c. 6,200 lectures. English titles can be found under http://www.rudolfsteinerweb.com/Rudolf_Steiner_Works.php.

PREFACE

After having given birth to my daughter 41 years ago, a pregnant friend of mine visited me in the hospital and brought me as a gift the book "Geburt und Kindheit" (Birth and Childhood) written by the anthroposophical physician Wilhelm zur Linden. While reading it, I spontaneously and consistently wanted to make the anthroposophical ideas the basis of my life. Since then, I have been deepening my knowledge about Rudolf Steiner's life and work. I found and still find endless revelations of spiritual science in his lectures. My interest for anthroposophical pedagogy, nourishment, medicine etc. grew. During my daughter's visiting the Waldorf Kindergarten and Rudolf Steiner School, I took pleasure in participating in diverse events (e. g. bazaars, orchestra, eurythmy, family leisure times).

My wish to know more about anthroposophy brought me to a manuscript which, after three years, led to the German book title "Ein Bau erobert die Welt – Das Goetheanum als Symbol der Anthroposophie", published in 2021. Two years later I felt the need to translate it into English which resulted in the first edition. My endeavour was to give the readers English references of most of the cited lectures of Rudolf Steiner.

My thanks go to Mr. Herbert Lippmann who accompanied the German version of this book by careful review of the manuscript and enriching comments. The English edition was supported by him with encouraging words.

This revised second edition I owe with great thanks to John Paull, PhD – University of Tasmania. After I had sent him a book of the first edition, he copyedited it on a three-hour flight from Hobart to Brisbane. After three Skype sessions from Tasmania to Germany this second edition ensued.

I am very grateful to my daughter Clarissa who took charge of design and layout for "The Triumph of Spirit".

May the lecture of this book arouse the interest in Anthroposophy and provide leisure times to those who are familiar with this spiritual science.

Munich, Michalmas 2023
Angelika Dorothea Albrecht

Note: Taking into account that the universal English language, besides the mother tongue, is also spoken in practically any part of the world, I was motivated to translate my book about the Goetheanum building into English. I obtained the knowledge of this language in 1959 in England with the *Lower Certificate in English* at the University of Cambridge, and in 1961 with the *Certificate in Training Course for Interpreters in English* at the Atlas Sprachschule in Nuremberg, Germany.

Introduction

«At the beginning of his anthroposophical career around the year 1900, Rudolf Steiner at first worked with small groups and individuals. In his autobiography he describes the preparatory phases in early scripts and in some letters. He worked with an independent German branch, which had originally emanated from the Theosophical Society. He did not take all of the conceptions and principles of the Indian tinged Theosophy, but created his own concept, calling it Anthroposophy, based on direct experiences with the spiritual world and spiritual creatures, thus laying the fundaments of a spiritual science of anthroposophical orientation – the Anthroposophical Society.»[1]

The visions arising from man's soul enabled him to replicate into the visible the reflection of supersensuality. Asked by one of his students which of his publications he regards the most important, Rudolf Steiner accordingly answered: «The Philosophy of Freedom. To internalize this book means to gain the knowledge of science of the mind with which one gets ahead in life even in a period of hundred years.» Rudolf Steiner wrote this philosophical main work in the year of 1894.[2]

Already in 1902, in a small series of lectures, Rudolf Steiner spoke about "Practical Karma Studies". He explained that not only the aspects of spirit and soul but also the energy of physical organs can have an impact on repeated lives on earth as deflecting forces. Man brings the latter ones from antenatal life to earth life and carry them over to postmortal life. In his last series of over eighty esoteric lectures which he gave before his death in 1925 he also applied himself to reflections on karma.[3] In this way, human destiny is subject of beginning and end of Rudolf Steiner's lecture themes.

1   **Pfeiffer, Ehrenfried** in his autobiography "A Modern Quest for the Spirit (1899 - 1961)" – Mercury Press, 2010. By courtesy of: Perseus Publishing House (translation from German 3rd edition), Basel 2003 (p. 109) – Postfach 611, CH-4144 Arlesheim, E-mail: kontakt@perseus.ch.
2   **Steiner, Rudolf:** "The Philosophy of Freedom: The Basis for a Modern World Conception" (CW 4) – Rudolf Steiner Press, 2011.
3   id.: "Karmic Relationships: Esoteric Studies" (CW 235 - CW 240) – Rudolf Steiner Press, 2009.

Also in 1902, in his course "Christianity as Mystical Fact: And the Mysteries of Antiquity"[1] Rudolf Steiner spoke of the nature of Christendom and its history of spirituality in the development of mankind. From 1913 till 1914 he gave ten lectures in his course "Approaching the Mystery of Golgotha".[2] He recited that by Christ's life, death and resurrection, the fulfilment and at the same time overcoming of the ancient mysteries are accomplished. Without the "Mystery of Golgotha" the ego of mankind's development would have got lost.

Rudolf Steiner's course, "An Outline of Esoteric Science"[3], first published in 1910, is one of his masterpieces about nature and development of mankind und its belonging to a cosmos which itself is in development. This volume remains the most comprehensive and effective presentation of a spiritual alternative to contemporary, materialistic cosmologies and offers new aspects to the Darwinian view of human nature and evolution.

The starting point was the philosophical idealism of the 19th century, mostly Johann Wolfgang Goethe's[4] philosophy of life. The used method was to observe spirit and its appearances and to describe the results. It was clear that this method of observation was different to that of the physical world. What is not accessible to the physical, three dimensional, ponderable and measurable world by material instruments and analyses requires spiritual sense organs.

The plan to erect a building which corresponds with an anthroposophical working place became reality in 1913. «Now you will call a building Goetheanum which has been erected in its architecture and plastic art with the intention to realize in its form the understanding of Goethe's view of metamorphose and to try to bring it to reality. (…) He who gets access to the thought of transformation not only by vivid physical forms (…) but also makes accessible the detectable by spirit and

1   Steiner, Rudolf: "Christianity as Mystical Fact: And the Mysteries of Antiquity" (CW 8) – Steiner-Books Inc, 1997.
2   id.: "Approaching the Mystery of Golgatha" (CW 152) – Anthroposophic Press Inc; illstr. ed., 2006.
3   id.: "An Outline of Esoteric Science. Classics by Rudolf Steiner" (CW 13) – Anthroposophic Press, 1997. By courtesy of: Perseus Publishing House (translation from German 3rd edition), Basel 2003 (p. 122/133).
4   Goethe, Johann Wolfgang von (1749 - 1832) was a German poet, playwright, novelist, scientist, statesman, anatomist and inventor of a new science of colour perception. He is widely regarded as universal genius and the greatest and most influential writer in the German language. Besides, his work had a profound and wide-ranging influence on western literary, political, and philosophical thoughts from the late 18th century to the present day. In 1782 he was ennobled ("von") by the emperor Joseph II.

soul, has arrived at Anthroposophy.» These were the words of Rudolf Steiner in his course "Architecture: As a Synthesis of the Arts"[1]. In eight lectures, he spoke of the origin of architecture arising from man's soul and his relationship to mankind's development (1911, 1913 and 1914).

Rudolf Steiner was conscious of how important art is and how much it can vitalize and relieve man's thinking. That's why – together with Marie Steiner von Sivers and other artists – in connection with his series of lectures and courses as well as conferences, he created time and again a new artistic frame for the audience by recitations, stage and eurythmy presentations and also musical performances.

«Until World War I, Anthroposophy gradually had developed to a perfect philosophy of life serving to renew mysteries and spiritually based art. The first Goetheanum building in Dornach became the physical centre of this philosophy of life. World War I (1914 - 1918) implicated a complete turnover of all human affairs and situations. Many people began to realize that materialism as philosophy and science perhaps may not be an answer to human, social and cultural problems of the world. Numerous values have been destroyed. The best, enthusiastic and hopeful youth were dead. And there also arouse the social question: How to organize human society? The political solutions which were undertaken, e. g. the Peace Treaty of Versailles, only lead to new conflicts and another war, as history shows. Man's old wound in social life burst. And when Marxism flooded Europe like a ground swell, Rudolf Steiner had the courage to articulate and demonstrate that this kind of socialism was an antisocial appearance.»[2]

At that point of time, the phase of practical application of Anthroposophy in the fields of science, medicine, schools, social life, agriculture and economy begins.

---

1   **Steiner, Rudolf:** "Architecture: As a Synthesis of the Arts" (CW 286) – Rudolf Steiner Press, 1999 (CW 175) – Rudolf Steiner Press, 2015.
2   **Pfeiffer, Ehrenfried:** "A Modern Quest for the Spirit (1899 - 1961)" – Mercury Press, 2010. By courtesy of: Perseus Verlag (translation from German 3rd edition), Basel 2003 (p. 112/113).

The esoterical impulse – Ehrenfried Pfeiffer called it "the Dornach impulse" – finally lead to the re-establishment of the Anthroposophical Society. The foundation celebrities took place on the 24th of December 1923, and numerous guests from near and far came to Switzerland to meet in the provisionally enlarged carpenter's workshop on the Dornach hill. In his entrance speech, Rudolf Steiner informed the audience of the statutes of the Allgemeine Anthroposophische Gesellschaft – AAG (General Anthroposophical Society). One year after the first Goetheanum building was burned down on New Year's Eve 1922/23, Rudolf Steiner postulated that «… it is the central point of all efforts for the Anthroposophical Society to foster anthroposophic spiritual science with its results for brotherhood in human living concerning moral, religious, artistic and general spiritual life.»

From that time on, Rudolf Steiner is Chairman of the Society; until then he had been its spiritual scientific teacher and lecturer without function in the Society; he even was not official member. Now he created a Board of Management with his active leadership to get decisive influence on the matters of the Society.

The foundation of the General Anthroposophical Society took place in a consecration act with a foundation motto of Rudolf Steiner which he recited at the beginning and at the end of the Christmas Conference 1923/24.[1] Its last rhyme reads as follows:

Divine light	*Enlighten*	*From our hearts,*
Sun of Christ,	*Our brains,*	*What our brains*
Warm	*So that good may become,*	*Will achieve*
Our hearts,	*What we establish*	*To reach the goal.*

According to Ehrenfried Pfeiffer it is a malicious distortion and rude allegation of adversaries to designate Anthroposophy as cult, sect or mysticism.

---

1   **Steiner, Rudolf:** "The Christmas Conference for the Foundation of the General Anthroposophical Society 1923/1924" (CW 260) – SteinerBooks, 2020.

Rudolf Josef Lorenz Steiner Ph.D.

*27.02.1861 Donji Kraljevec
Austro-Hungarian Empire (now in Croatia)
† **30.03.1925 Dornach** (Switzerland)

- Studies at Vienna University of Technology;
- Doctor of Philosophy 1891 in Rostock. Title "The Basic Question of Epistemology" (science of knowledge).

Founder of
- a new spiritual science, called "Anthroposophy"
- the Anthroposophical Society with the Freie Hochschule für Geisteswissenschaft am Goetheanum (School of Spiritual Science at the Goetheanum)
- the Social Threefolding
- the Threefolding of Man
- Eurythmy (a new art of movement for voice, speech, healing and education)
- anthroposophic enhanced medicine and pharmacy (co-founder of Weleda AG)
- the biodynamic agriculture
- the Waldorf education movement

Fig. 1   Rudolf Steiner (1908)[1]

Advisor
- for the movement of religious renewal – "Die Christengemeinschaft" (The Christian Community)

Innovator
- of pedagogical art
- of science of nutrition

Creator of a new
- art of painting
- architecture
- stagecraft

RECOMMENDATIONS FOR FURTHER LITERATURE

Selg, Peter: "Rudolf Steiner: Life and Work" – SteinerBooks Inc, 2014
- 1861 - 1890 Childhood, Youth, and Study Years.
- 1890 - 1900 Weimar and Berlin.
- 1900 - 1914 Spiritual Science & Spiritual Community.
- 1914 - 1918 The Years of World War I.
- 1919 - 1922 Social Threefolding and the Waldorf School.
- 1923 The Burning of the Goetheanum.
- 1924 - 1925 The Anthroposophical Society and the School for Spiritual Science.
Steiner, Rudolf: "The Story of My Life 1861 - 1907" (CW 28) – Anthroposophic Press Inc, 2005
Wachsmuth, Guenther: "The Life and Work of Rudolf Steiner: From the Turn of the Century to his Death" – SteinerBooks Inc, 1995.

[1]   **Steiner, Rudolf:** (1908): Photo Fig. 1 (cutout) and life dates by courtesy of: Stiftung Kulturimpuls, Deutsches Stiftungszentrum, Barkhovenallee 1, 45239 Essen, Germany.

Chapter 1

The First Goetheanum Building on the Dornach Hill

We can estimate joys in the presence, but sufferings only in the future.
The first ones are gifts of good laws, but the latters are teachers of wisdom.
To suffer goes along with a higher development.
It is that what you can't dispense with to come to knowledge.[1]

Rudolf Steiner (1861 - 1925)

As of 1911 the managing board of the Anthroposophical Society – had been trying to obtain the permission to erect the planned "Johannes Building" in Munich. A building model was already made in 1908/09 after the ideas of Rudolf Steiner by Ernst August Karl Stockmeyer[2] together with his father, the painter Karl Stockmeyer.

But before the Munich Building Commission at the end of February 1913 again declined this building project, Rudolf Steiner and Marie Steiner von Sivers – after having finished the lecture course on the Mark gospel in Basel, Switzerland in autumn 1912 – were guests of Nelly and Emil Grosheintz-Laval (doctor in dental science D.D.S.)[3] in their isolated House Brodbeck on the Dornach hill. This location, erected in 1905 as summer residence for Nelly and Emil, is now Rudolf Steiner Halde. Marie Steiner von Sivers later reported that Rudolf Steiner awoke the other morning «disturbed, like crushed, completely gloomy, what otherwise did never happen, because despite eternal rush he lived in harmony». Marie Steiner von Sivers had the feeling that «in this night he had a presentiment of disaster which he had to forbid himself to think of».

---

1 **Steiner, Rudolf:** "The Spiritual Hierarchies and their Reflection in the Physical World" (CW 110) – Anthroposophic Press, 1970.
2 **Stockmeyer, E. A. K.** (1886 - 1936) was co-founder and teacher of the first Waldorf School in Stuttgart in 1919.
3 **Grosheintz-Laval, Emil,** D.D.S. (1867 - 1946) was co-founder and member of the managing board of the Swiss Anthroposophical Paracelsus branch. He was bestman at the wedding of Rudolf Steiner and Marie von Sivers. He took part in the event of the foundation stone of the first Goetheanum building and the first medical course of Rudolf Steiner. He sometimes accompanied Rudolf Steiner on his lecture tours.

In the course of this visit, Emil Grosheintz-Laval generously offered to Rudolf Steiner as a present this huge property to have erected the planned Johannes Building on the Dornach hill. Later on, the Swiss Building Authority in Basel generously permitted this building which – in appreciation of Johann Wolfgang von Goethe – was renamed "Goetheanum" in 1913.

The first Goetheanum building looked as if it were of stone. But – except the concrete base – it was of wood and plaster. Its total volume amounted to 66,000 cubic meters. It existed only two years – as of 1920 till 1922. On New Year's Eve 1922/1923 the building was destroyed by fire.

Peter Selg, M.D., formulated the following: «Taking into account all the gossips and publications in the surroundings of the catholic priest Maximilian Kully[1] of Arlesheim and others from 1920 versus the Goetheanum building, Steiner and Anthroposophy, with all that hate, fury and appeals of destruction – continuously increasing until the night of the fire – it is a clear incitement emotionally but also physically.»[2]

«From the beginning of the Goetheanum's construction till its completion, Rudolf Steiner, year by year, was in Dornach for a longer time to observe its realization. Besides he accepted invitations to hold courses and lectures in numerous towns of Europe. Their preparation, research and elaboration required such an intensive occupation by abundance of content that it would have been already a full-time job for another person. Furthermore, he welcomed from early to late a never-ending queue of people seeking advice, asking him for solutions of personal-human or scientific problems. With every visitor in uninterrupted order from all fields of life and knowledge, he was asked questions which often concerned the destiny of a person, the progress of a research work, the introduction of far-reaching measures.

But he also devoted his time to personally advising his students how to continue their esoteric education. Furthermore, he had to cope with numerous obligations concerning organisation and administration. (…)

1   **Kully, Maximilian** (1878 - 1936): Swiss catholic priest in Arlesheim from 1913 till 1936 who was known as public adversary of Rudolf Steiner.
2   **Selg, Peter**, M.D. (born 1963) is pediatrician, psychiatrist and psychologist for children and young people; he is director of the "Ita Wegman Institut" in Arlesheim, Switzerland, professor of medical Anthroposopy at the German Alanus College for Art and Society and leading physician at the "Klinik Arlesheim".

Fig. 2   The first Goetheanum building. Topping out ceremony, 1st of April, 1914.[1]

In addition, Rudolf Steiner cared about his written, scientific and literary publications which appeared year after year. And he even found time and energy to read a lot of books pertaining to science, art, history, literature etc. In conversations one could evermore only be amazed and perplexed about his large knowledge of former and today's current phenomena.»[2]

1   Photo Fig. 2: O. Rietmann. By courtesy of: "Rudolf Steiner Archiv", Dornach.
2   **Wachsmuth, Guenther** "The Life and Work of Rudolf Steiner" – SteinerBooks, 1995. Quotation by courtesy of: Philosophisch-Anthroposophischer Verlag am Goetheanum, Dornach 1951 (p. 360).

Fig. 3 The first Goetheanum building, completed in 1922.[1]

By additional purchase, the site meanwhile had a size of 12 hectares. As a second architect, Rudolf Steiner engaged Ernst Aisenpreis (1884 - 1949), 30 years of age at that time. Many young people from different countries who were committed to Anthroposophy with heart, body and soul and who had personally met Rudolf Steiner on the occasion of his numerous lectures in Germany, Austria-Hungary[2], England, Norwegian, Russia, France, the Netherlands were attracted to Dornach in order to contribute to the erection of the Goetheanum building. Among them were writers, composers, painters, actors, eurythmists, stage technicians, physicians and others. In Rudolf Steiner's near personal vicinity there were 18 people from about 17 countries who – in the interim or in the long term – lived and worked in Dornach. They felt as students and protectors of their highly esteemed and beloved "Doctor".

---

1   Photo Fig. 3: © Keystone.
2   A united monarchy of the emperor of Austria and the king of Hungary with Bosnia (1867 - 1915).

«In 1919 the shell of the first Goetheanum building was almost finished. The coloured glass windows – manufactured according to the principle of the flexible wave and artfully worked with a grinding wheel – were inserted. Now, as World War I was over, the technical construction, artistic and plastic works could be continued more intensively and quicker with a larger staff. Rudolf Steiner – in every hour which was not needed for lectures and meetings – was present at the building site, in the carpenter's workshop and on the scaffolds where artists worked sculpting and/or painting the two imposing cupolas. Besides leading, correcting and helping he carved and painted himself.»[1]

The first performance of the "Christmas Plays from Oberufer"[2] in front of an audience was prepared.

The problems of stage construction, lighting, and ventilation were discussed all night long.

Then began the intensive cooperation with Rudolf Steiner regarding stage design and art of eurythmy created with Marie Steiner von Sivers. The actors of his four mystery dramas[3] should be surrounded – according to the mood content of the spoken word – with constantly fluctuating and fully coloured space. Fortunately, Rudolf Steiner's instructions for the lighting could be saved. But the harmony of architecture, performance of the light being reflected on wood, the painting of the double cupola, and most intensive colour flood coordinated with that what happened on stage could not be reproduced after the first Goetheanum building was burned down to its foundation.

1 Grosse, Rudolf: "The Christmas Foundation" – SteinerBooks, 1984. "Die Weihnachtstagung als Zeitenwende". Quotations by courtesy of: Philosophisch-Anthroposophischer Verlag Goetheanum, Dornach, Schweiz 1976 (p. 77).
2 Steiner, Rudolf: "Christmas Plays from Oberufer" – Rudolf Steiner Press; illustr. ed., 2007.
The Paradise Play, acting as a preface, presents the expulsion of Adam and Eve from paradise, but with the promise of future salvation through Christ. The Shepherds Play portrays the birth of Jesus in a stable, where he is sought out by a group of shepherds. The Kings Play depicts the visit of three wise kings to the birthplace of the King of Humanity, as well as the murderous attempts by Herod to thwart Jesus' mission. Between 1915 and 1924, Rudolf Steiner hold 18 addresses to the audience of the Christmas Plays. The German CW number is GA 274.
3 id.: "Four Mystery Dramas: The Portal of Initiation – The Soul's Probation – The Guardian of the Threshold – The Soul's Awakening: The Portal of Initiation" (CW 14) – SteinerBooks, 1973.
The first drama deals with Rosicrution mystery. The second gives a life tableau in dramatic scenes as sequel to the first play. The third and fourth play deals with soul events in dramatic scenes. The four mystery plays had their annual premiere in Munich in rotation from 1910 till 1913. Quotation of Rudolf Steiner in the same volume: «If I had only created these four mystery dramas, they would contain the whole substance of Anthroposophy.»

The two copper dodecahedrons of the foundation stone with a length of 96 cm. Inside there are two hung floating pyrite crystals; in the bigger body a smaller one, in the larger a smaller, demonstrating a mirror image to the double cupola. In the inside is kept safely the document of the foundation stone drawn by Rudolf Steiner and signed by all members present. This foundation stone was used as fundament for the first and second Goetheanum building.

The place of the foundation stone is below the place where, later on, was erected the teacher's desk.

In 1913 this stone became the fundament of the Goetheanum building. In a solemn ceremony in 1923, Rudolf Steiner connected it once again with the hearts of all members around the whole world.

Fig. 4   Foundation stone of the Goetheanum building.[1]

Rudolf Steiner described the Goetheanum building «as a symbol of our movement» and designated it to guarantee this loyalty, this uncompromising attitude, this uninterrupted spiritual continuity in times of war, peace and in most difficult ages.[2]

On 20th of September 1913 the solemnly laying of the foundation stone on the Dornach hill took place. During a lecture on the occasion of this event Rudolf Steiner said the following words: «From all sides will emerge toad natures that will take offense and feel irritated. Therefore, we will have to be extremely attentive and need to stand on guard!»

1   Photo: Max Benzinger (cover of the conference flyer). By courtesy of: "Rudolf Steiner Archiv", Dornach.
2   **Steiner, Rudolf**: "The Aims of Anthroposophy and the Purpose of the Goetheanum" (CW 84) – Rudolf Steiner Press, 2020.

«The motto of the foundation stone (see page 13) was a three-piece meditation of man's nature. These quotations are heard, received and spoken through words that are revealed to the world. (…) The ground into which the foundation stone was sunk represented the hearts of the attendees in their harmonic interaction, in their will imbued with love to carry together the anthroposophic want through the world.»[1]

The night before New Year's Eve in 1922, when the first Goetheanum building with all its beauty and treasures was burned down to its foundation plinth, also parts of Rudolf Steiner's nature and physicality were destroyed. Ten years of his life with all the hopes, targets, creative work were erased in the course of a few hours. One could see the fire's shine in a distance of about 50 kilometres up to the Black Forest, the Suisse Jura Mountains and Vosges. It could not be confirmed judicially whether the cause was a question of arson. Yet, Rudolf Steiner often had pointed to the necessity to protect the building because, already before the fire broke out, a local catholic priest directed flaming attacks against him and the Goetheanum building.

In the vicinity of the Goetheanum building there were located the carpenter's workshop, temporarily the small stage, the lecture hall and also Rudolf Steiner's studio in which he worked, together with his faithful assistant Miss Edith Maryon, to complete the timber sculpture "Christ as Representative of Mankind Between Lucifer and Ahriman". Sparks of the huge fire fell onto the roof of the carpenter's workshop, so the main efforts during this night were to rescue this building and the studio.

Later on, after everybody had been called away from the place of fire, Ehrenfried Pfeiffer found Rudolf Steiner and Edith Maryon overlooking the area. «Known by the crowd as a big teacher of spiritual wisdom, a creator of new arts, an esoteric teacher or initiated person, a clairvoyant who was able to bring secrets from the spiritual world to earth – obviously nobody could imagine that Rudolf Steiner also was a man who could suffer, had feelings, who needed comfort at the moment of heaviest despair, whose heart was broken in this night. (…) I realized the spiritual loneliness of this great man. In my heart arose a vow to never leave him neither his work nor his person.»[2]

It gives evidence of the knowledge of indestructibility and continuous creativity with regard to the essence of anthroposophic spiritual science

1   **Wachsmuth, Guenther:** "The Life and Work of Rudolf Steiner" – SteinerBooks, 1995. Quotation by courtesy of: Philosophisch-Anthroposophischer Verlag am Goetheanum, Dornach 1951 (p. 384).
2   **Ehrenfried Pfeiffer:** "A Modern Quest for the Spirit (1899 - 1961)" – Mercury Press, 2010. By courtesy of: Perseus Verlag (translation from German 3rd edition), Basel 2003 (p. 102 ff).

that Rudolf Steiner incited his students on the same day to perform the "Three Kings Play" in the provisionally prepared carpenter's workshop.

After the Goetheanum building was burned down, Rudolf Steiner repeatedly referred to the fire of the Greek Artemis Temple in Ephesus in 356 B. C. which is known to have fallen victim to arson. He described the spiritual impact on physical destruction that enabled a stronger relocation of the corresponding power structures in the ether substance of earth.

And in a lecture on 9th April of 1923 in Basel, Rudolf Steiner spoke of the «terrible fire catastrophe of the past New Year's Eve in which the first Goetheanum building was destroyed: »The building was for the eye what Anthroposophy should be for man's soul.»[1]

In accordance with Rudolf Steiner, it was Guenther Wachsmuth who organized a new group of guardians who guaranteed the protection of the remaining fundaments of the building by day and night in order to save it for calmer times. Thirty young persons took over this sacrificial task like others had done already during the erection of the first Goetheanum building. Many of them could notice how long Rudolf Steiner worked in his studio and that the light was turned off only for few hours, often only for one hour.

The wooden model "Christ as the Representative of Humanity between Lucifer and Ahriman" (see Fig. 5) with a height of eight metres was designed by Rudolf Steiner and – together with the English sculptor Edith Maryon[2] – was created for the first Goetheanum building in Dornach from 1915 till 1924/25. Rudolf Steiner spoke about this work in five lectures, published in different volumes.[3] It was planned to have it set up in the small cupola room, the first stage room of the building. It was not yet finished when, on New Year's Eve of 1922/23, the building was burned down. The model stood in the studio of the carpenter's workshop and, therefore, it was spared from destruction. Before it could be finished, both of its creators died: Edith Maryon in 1924 and Rudolf Steiner in 1925.

1 **Steiner, Rudolf:** "The Aims of Anthroposophy and the Purpose of the Goetheanum" (CW 84) – Rudolf Steiner Press, 2020.
2 **Selg, Peter:** "Edith Maryon: Rudolf Steiner and the Sculpture of Christ in Dornach" – Temple Lodge Publishing, 2023.
3 **Steiner, Rudolf:** "The Mystery of Death" 1915 (GA 159) – No English edition. "Dying Earth and Living Cosmos: The Living Gifts of Anthroposophy" 1918 (CW 181) – Rudolf Steiner Press, 2014. "Michael's Mission: Revealing the Essential Secrets of Human Nature" 1920 (CW 194) – Rudolf Steiner Press, 2016. "The Fourth Dimension – Sacred Geometry, Alchemy and Mathematics" 1904 (CW 324a) – SteinerBooks, Inc; 2001.

Fig. 5 "Christ as Representative of Mankind Between Lucifer and Ahriman".[1]

1   Photo by courtesy of: "Rudolf Steiner Archiv", Dornach, Switzerland.

Chapter 2

The Anthroposophic Movement

We have to feel spiritual presence in persuing Anthroposophy.[1]

Rudolf Steiner (1861 - 1925)

After having methodically developed Anthroposophy, Rudolf Steiner consequently established the anthroposophical spiritual science[2]. While the science of principally naturally orientated anthropology only describes man as externally comprehensible, Anthroposophy will also empirically research how man can also be conceived only by inside experience which enables him by consequent awareness training to realize the worlds of soul and spirit.

In July of 1923, after the first Goetheanum building was burned down, Rudolf Steiner prepared the realization of the second Goetheanum building with the Congress for Members and Delegates from all over the world. After having carried out the administrative negotiations regarding the fire, insurance, re-erection, Rudolf Steiner took over the performance of the new building again according to his own drafts and guidelines and creating the model with his own hands. He concluded the congress with the words: «… And it would be fine if this new Goetheanum could beam towards us what should be said to mankind on the basis of Anthroposophy.» One month before, at the general meeting of the Society's association, Rudolf Steiner expressed «… that we, under no circumstances, will abandon the continuity of the work of our spiritual life. (…) That we work from the centre of spirituality and don't allow ourselves to be deterred by anything. (…) This is the prerequisite for the anthroposophic movement's real perspective.»

At the 1923/24 Christmas Conference of the Anthroposophical Society, Rudolf Steiner re-established the Society. He assumed the difficult leadership of the Allgemeine Anthroposophische Gesellschaft – AAG (General Anthroposophical Society) and of the Freie Hochschule für Geisteswissenschaft (School of Spiritual Science).

---

1   **Steiner, Rudolf:** "The Spiritual Hierarchies and their Reflection in the Physical World" (CW 110) – Anthroposophic Press, 1970.
2   **id.:** "The Philosophy of Freedom" (CW 4) – Lulu.com, 2011.

Fig. 6   Blackboard drawing of Rudolf Steiner in Torquay, England (August 1924).[1]

The 800 representative participants were informed that Rudolf Steiner «… who, until then had been the Society's spiritual scientific teacher, will now take over the leadership of the Society and School also with their burdens and human imperfection together with a managing board of five members who should represent the Society in its different streams.» (See also Chapter 10).

«On this morning, Rudolf Steiner spoke words dressed with the wings of angels and hierarchies from whom they originated. It was the laying of the foundation stone he placed into the hearts of the members.»[2]

In his German book "The Christmas Conference as Turning Point", Rudolf Grosse (1905 - 1994)[3] wrote the following enlightening lines: «At the Christmas Conference (from 23rd of December 1922 till 1st of January 1923), the Goetheanum in Dornach has become the centre of the Anthroposophical Society. If this building had not been destroyed, these days of highest spiritual consecration had been its inauguration. The Goetheanum, in such a comprehensive way represented by the supernaturally real events of these nine days, emanated a kind of a mystery consecration. And Rudolf Steiner as its creator – once of the physical building, now of the spiritual building of

1   Photo by courtesy of: "Rudolf Steiner Archiv", Dornach, Switzerland.
2   **Poeppig, Fred**: "Destiny Paths to Rudolf Steiner" – J. Ch. Mellinger, Stuttgart 1955.
3   **Grosse, Rudolf**: "Die Weihnachtstagung als Zeitenwende". Quotations by courtesy of: Philosophisch-Anthroposophischer Verlag Goetheanum, Dornach, Switzerland 1976 (p. 77) – Rudolf Grosse was Waldorf teacher and member of the managing board of the General Anthroposophical Society as well as Head of the Youth Section and Pedagogic Section at the Goetheanum.

mankind – was no longer the same person. In independent spiritual sover-
eignty he had undertaken a double task that in former cultural epochs could
not have been connected, for the laws of the spiritual world, in the strictest
ways guarded by Archangel Michael, do not give space for the combination
of two tasks because they mutually exclude themselves. (…) However, in
being confronted with the iron necessity to take over both of the areas of
responsibility, Rudolf Steiner could do this – according to his own words –
only to make a promise towards the spiritual world.»

In one of eleven lectures, Rudolf Steiner gave more insights about this statement to the English members of the Anthroposophical Society who attended the
International Summer School in August 1924 in Torquay, England. This meeting
was organized by his friend and colleague D. N. Dunlop[1]. Rudolf Steiner also
explained to the audience his blackboard drawing *Human/Animal/Plant*: "As a
human being, I carry in me the physical, mental, spiritual world".[2]

In another lecture[3] on the occasion of Edith Maryon's cremation in Basel
on the 6th of May 1924 Rudolf Steiner expressed himself with the following
words: «The management of the anthroposophic movement necessitates that I
am myself in the position to carry up to the spiritual world that what happens
to me in order not only to fulfil a responsibility towards anything on the physical plan but a responsibility that absolutely goes up to the spiritual worlds. You
see, ladies and gentlemen, if you want to participate in the right sense in that
what the anthroposophic movement has become since the Christmas Conference, you have to make yourselves confident with this thought what it means
to make the anthroposophic movement accountable to the spiritual world.»

1   **Dunlop, Daniel Nicol** (1868 - 1935) met Rudolf Steiner in 1922. It was the Dutch manager Joseph
    van Leer who brought them together. They sat at the table together – Rudolf Steiner who spoke
    no English and D. N. Dunlop who spoke no German. Joseph van Leer stepped in as translator but
    what he didn't see was that Rudolf Steiner took the hand of Daniel Dunlop and held it, under the
    table, during the whole of the conversation. In 1934, during one of his famous Summer Schools,
    Dunlop shared the memory of this with his friend Walter Johannes Stein. He made an even more
    interesting statement, that Rudolf Steiner on this occasion had said to him: «We are brothers».
    Eleanor Merry, also an active member of the early British Anthroposophical Society, worked
    intensively with Dunlop for the last 14 years of his life during which time he told her that Rudolf
    Steiner gave him an insight into a former life of his where he, Dunlop, had been a member of the
    innermost circle of the Order of the Knights Templar.
2   **Steiner, Rudolf**: "True and False Paths of Spiritual Research" (CW 243) – Rudolf Steiner Press,
    2009. Picture by courtesy of: "Rudolf Steiner Archiv", Dornach, Switzerland.
3   id.: "Our Dead: Memorial, Funeral, and Cremation Addresses 1906 - 1924 (with two lectures in
    Kassel)" (CW 261) – SteinerBooks Inc; illustr. ed., 2011.

Chapter 3

DESTINY PATHS TO DORNACH

It has to be drawn attention to the fact that anthroposophic spiritual science has the mission to especially introduce into life, to incorporate into life, what comes from a soul which bit by bit gets the conviction that the ideas of karma and reincarnation are reality.[1]

Rudolf Steiner (1861 - 1925)

In the beginning of the 20th century many people who were looking for a spiritual life found their path to Dornach, Switzerland. Most of them had become acquainted with Anthroposophy and Rudolf Steiner by his lectures in numerous towns of Europe. Some immediately followed him, others later. Many of them met again in Dornach and helped there to erect the first Goetheanum building forming a special community whilst World War I raged outside of Switzerland. «Rudolf Steiner led this group of people to a reality of a community that embodied itself creating its purposeful life laws by spiritual and practical work.»[2]

Hermann Linde
Painter

* 26.08.1863 Lübeck (Germany)
† 26.06.1923 Arlesheim (Switzerland)

Abb. 7   Self portrait[3]

1   **Steiner, Rudolf** (1912) in: "Reincarnation and Karma: Two Fundamental Truths of Human Existence" (CW 135) – Anthroposophic Press, 2001.
2   **Wachsmuth, Guenther:** "The Life and Work of Rudolf Steiner", SteinerBooks 1995. Quotation by courtesy of: Philosophisch-Anthroposophischer Verlag am Goetheanum, Dornach 1951 (p. 360).
3   **Linde, Hermann:** "Self portrait", c. 1910 – https://de. Wikipedia.org/wiki/Hermann_Linde_(Maler).

Fig. 8 Cross-section through both cupola halls of the first Goetheanum building with view of the ceiling paintings of the small cupola (left) and large cupola (right). It showed numerous motifs of mankind's spiritual history.[1]

In the post-war turmoil many of those people were again spread to all winds. Some stayed forever. The following short biographies represent only a selection. Their order ensues by calendar dates of birth.

The father of Hermann Linde[2] was a pharmacist and the renowned photographer Hermann Linde senior. His brothers were the ophthalmologist and art collector Max Linde und the painter Heinrich Eduard Linde-Walther. His grandfather, a decorative art painter, gave first drawing lessons to the young Hermann Linde.

Until 1889 he studied at the Dresden and Weimar academies. In 1890 he undertook study trips to Sicily, Egypt and Tunisia. From 1892 till 1895 he worked as free-lance painter in India. For two years he had been living in the artist colony in Dachau, Germany. He was honoured with numerous awards and prizes.

---

1   Photo Fig. 8: https://anthrowiki.at/Die_Deckenmalerei_der_gro%C3%9Fen_Kuppel_des_ersten_
     Goetheanums.
2   Adapted text by courtesy of: Stiftung Kulturimpuls, Deutsches Stiftungszentrum, Barkhovenallee 1,
     45239 Essen, Germany.

After having met Rudolf Steiner in 1910, at the age of 47, Hermann Linde followed the anthroposophic movement. Rudolf Steiner entrusted him with the interior painting of the first Goetheanum building. Hermann Linde was supported by Wilhelm Nedella (1886 - 1941). He also made sketches of Rudolf Steiner's lecture course "Goethe's Spirituality: As Revealed by Faust" and "The Fairy Tale of the Green Snake and the Beautiful Lily".[1] Incited by Rudolf Steiner, Hermann Linde performed the fairy tale in a synopsis with motifs of the first mystery drama "The Portal of Initiation" which had its premiere in Munich's Playhouse in 1910.

Hermann Linde died half a year after the Goetheanum building was burned down on New Year's Eve of 1922/23. According to Rudolf Steiner he died of broken heart. He had connected his complete existence with the building and its inside paintings.

---

1   Steiner, Rudolf: "Goethe's Spirituality: As Revealed by Faust and The Fairy Tale of the Green Snake and the Beautiful Lily" (CW 22) – Independently Published, 2019.

Marie Steiner von Sivers

Artist, Member of the Foundation Board of the Allgemeine Anthroposophische Gesellschaft – AAG (General Anthroposophical Society), Head of the Section "Arts of Eurythmy, Speech, Drama and Music" of the Freie Hochschule für Geisteswissenschaft am Goetheanum (School of Spiritual Science at the Goetheanum).

* 14.03.1867 Wlotzlawek
  near Warschau (at that time Russia)
† 27.12.1948 Beatenberg (Switzerland)

Fig. 9   Marie von Sivers (c. 1902)[1]

Marie von Sivers was seven or eight years old when her father moved from Wlotzlawek to Riga, the capital of Latvia. Two years later he quit his military service and relocated to Russia (St. Petersburg). There, Marie von Sivers attended a German private school and strived to study linguistics and comparative religion which was not allowed by her conservative parents.

Yet, supported by her parents, Marie von Sivers took up studies of recitation and stage acting in Paris, France from 1895 till 1897 at the "Conservatoire de Paris". After having returned to St. Petersburg, she continued and deepened her studies of stage acting. In 1899 she was offered to play at Berlin's Schiller Theatre whereupon she moved to Germany.

From here she contacts Edouard Schuré[2] at the beginning of October 1900 and asks him for his permission to translate into German his first two dramas, to which he agrees.

Edouard Schuré draws her attention to the German Theosophic Society where in November 1900 – at the age of 33 – she met for the first time Rudolf Steiner who was invited there to give a lecture and who was in his 40th year of age.

---

1   Photo Fig. 9 and adapted text by courtesy of: Stiftung Kulturimpuls, Deutsches Stiftungszentrum, Barkhovenallee 1, 45239 Essen, Germany.

2   **Schuré, Edouard** (1841 - 1929): French writer and theosophist. His today's notoriety is based on his main work "The Great Initiates" (Garber Books, 1992), published in 1889. Moreover, he was author of dramas, novels, poems and different treatises about philosophy, history and music.

In her memoirs, Margarita Woloschin describes Marie von Sivers as follows: «She had golden hair and a complexion which was blooming and delicate like the skin of children. With amazing blue and fiery eyes like sapphires she looked at the world. Her mouth was soft but firm, the chin concise. Her beautiful small hands attracted my attention. She could heartily laugh or be outraged whereby the blood gently mounted into her face. (…) She was unapproachable like a queen, although she never put herself above others. She owned a childlike immediacy and a sparkling humor.»[1]

Though Rudolf Steiner was not a member of the Theosophic Society, few weeks later the leader of the Berlin branch asked Rudolf Steiner whether he might be prepared to take his place. But only after Marie von Sivers had accepted to be his assistant, Rudolf Steiner was ready to work for the Theosophic Society providing his knowledge of spiritual science.

In mid-January 1902, Rudolf Steiner became head of the Berlin branch and at the same time a member of the Theosophic Society. By the end of April, he was asked to take over also the function of a General Secretary on the occasion of the foundation of a planned German section. This took place in October 1902 with Marie von Sivers as managing director. She was the first person to realize the great importance of Rudolf Steiner who spoke from beyond the threshold separating death and life.

Because she was disposed of an independent spirituality, was energetic and highly educated, familiar with world literature, fluently spoke five languages and disposed of an extraordinary ability to devote herself to the cause, Marie von Sivers could keep pace with the overwhelming work performed by Rudolf Steiner.

In December 1911, Rudolf Steiner and Marie von Sivers "left" the Theosophic Society because of ideological differences. Marie von Sivers devoted herself to further develop and spread Anthroposophy as spiritual science. She organized the foundation of the Anthroposophical Society on 28th of December 1912 in Cologne, Germany as well as Rudolf Steiner's lecture journeys. In the beginning, the members amounted to 120 in 10 branches; in 1913 the number of members increased to 2,500 in 54 branches.

Marie von Sivers soon became an indispensable assistant and interpreter while accompanying Rudolf Steiner on his numerous lecture trips to different European countries. She started her own publishing company and took over

---

1   **Woloschin, Margarita:** "The Green Snake; An Autobiography" – Floris Books, 2010.

the organisation of stenographic transcriptions, printing and distribution of Rudolf Steiner's lectures which he always gave in extemporaneously speech. On the occasion of the Christmas Conference in 1923/24, when the Anthroposophical Society was re-established and Rudolf Steiner took over the leadership, also Marie von Sivers was nominated member of the managing board of the General Anthroposophical Society and head of the Section for Speech and Musical Art. Their mutual interest for poetry, for art of stage and speaking, later on also for eurythmy lead to the Munich Festival events of the years 1907 till 1913.

Marie von Sivers and Rudolf Steiner married on Christmas 1914. From that time on, she was addressed as "Frau Doktor Steiner".

After the end of World War I, as of 1919, she introduced to Europe's cultural life the new art of movement eurythmy by going on tour with the Dornach Eurythmy Ensemble. Thereby, eurythmy schools and anthroposophic art centres arose in various countries.

When, on New Year's Eve 1922/23, the first Goetheanum building was burned down and therefore the staging of the mystery dramas could not be realized, Rudolf Steiner was asked by young artists to give a course. Together with Marie Steiner von Sivers, in September 1924, Rudolf Steiner conducted the course "Speech and Drama" with 19 lectures[1]. In this way, the renewal of stage art was introduced. It was the last course of Rudolf Steiner, for immediately after he retired to his sickbed in his studio. At the feet of the timber sculpture "Christ as Representative of Mankind between Lucifer and Ahriman" at which he had worked until last, he was busy with writing and managing for another half of year. At the age of 64, Rudolf Steiner finally crossed the threshold of death. During his lifetime he dedicated numerous poems to his wife.

For the beloved Marie von Sivers

To build the word in your ego
To regard the ego in the worlds
Is breath of soul,
Cosmic experience.
In feeling selfhood
Is pulse of wisdom
And paths of spirit.

To describe one's own aim
Is language of truth.
And breath of soul penetrates
Into pulse of wisdom, releasing
From man's basics
The language of truth
In rhythms of life years.

Rudolf Steiner (15th March 1911)

---

1   **Steiner, Rudolf:** "Speech and Drama" (CW 282) – Anthroposophic Press Inc; illustr. ed., 1960.

Edith Maryon

Sculptor,
Head of the Section "Fine Arts"
of the Freie Hochschule für
Geisteswissenschaft am Goetheanum
(School of Spiritual Science at the
Goetheanum).

* 09.02.1872 **London** (UK)
† 01.05.1924 **Dornach** (Switzerland)

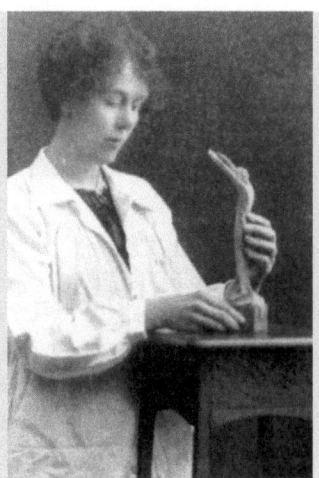

Fig. 10   Edith Maryon, creating a eurythmy figure.[1]

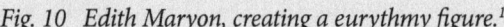

Edith Maryon was a successful sculptor and portraitist in England at the turn of 19th to 20th century. Together with Marie Steiner von Sivers and Ita Wegman she belonged to the closest co-workers of Rudolf Steiner. In Dornach, Switzerland she was a member of the first staff of the School of Spiritual Science at the Goetheanum in her functions as Head of the Section for Fine Arts and Vice President of the Anthroposophical Society. In cooperation with Rudolf Steiner, she performed the monumental wooden sculpture "Christ as Representative of Mankind between Lucifer and Ahriman" and also created numerous eurythmy figures as well as some models under Rudolf Steiner's patronage.

Edith Maryon's father was a tailor for London's high society. In the vicinity of her parents' house was located the British Museum where she could study the large collection of Egyptian, Greek and Roman sculptures. Later on, she attended an illustrious boarding school near Geneva, Switzerland. In the 1890s Edith Maryon studied sculpture at the London Central School of Design and in 1904, at the age of 32, she became "Associate" of the meanwhile renamed Royal College of Arts. She continued her studies by travelling to Assisi and Rome. Every now and then, her artworks – especially sculptures and reliefs – could be admired at exhibitions.

---

1   Photo Fig. 10 and adapted text by courtesy of: Stiftung Kulturimpuls, Deutsches Stiftungszentrum, Barkhovenallee 1, 45239 Essen, Germany.

Edith Maryon took interest in occult and spiritual things which was not uncommon in circles of artists at the beginning of the 20th century. In 1909 she joined the "Order of the Golden Dawn", called "Stella Matutina" (morning star) and for the first time came across the name of Rudolf Steiner. Because her two letters to him remained unanswered, she travelled to Germany where she attended in Berlin a lecture of Rudolf Steiner on 14th May of 1912. At the age of 40 – in a personal conversation with Rudolf Steiner – she decided to completely change her life. In August 1913 she took part in the third and fourth mystery dramas in Munich performing eurythmy with the Chorus of Gnomes and Sylphs. More and more she hoped to do something for the anthroposophic cause in using her abilities. She decides to leave England. However, at the beginning of 1914, this decision was seriously at stake; she fell badly ill. As for Edith Maryon's therapy, her English physician communicates with Rudolf Steiner. She recovers and moves to Dornach in the summer of the same year.

Talking about the Goetheanum building during his lecture journeys, Rudolf Steiner often describes Edith Maryon as example for the artistic commitment and the selfless dedication of the colleagues working on the erection of this anthroposophic building. She was the one who saved him from falling down a scaffold erected around the tall sculpture while both were working in a height of about six meters. It could have been Rudolf Steiner's death. How important this salvation was for the anthroposophic cause after 1916 can be explained by the following specification of Rudolf Steiner's activities: discovery of the threefold organism, foundation of all subordinate anthroposophic movements from medicine to pedagogy and agriculture, as well as the threefold social order, the foundation of the General Anthroposophical Society with the School of Spiritual Science, the special courses and lectures on karma.

During the last construction phase of the Goetheanum building, some of the staff expressed the wish to put the almost finished timber sculpture "Christ as Representative of Mankind between Lucifer and Ahriman" already at its central place in the building. But Rudolf Steiner and Edith Maryon agreed synonymously that this could wait. Consequently, this sculpture, representing the visible key message of Anthroposophy, did not fell prey to the flames of the fire which destroyed the first Goetheanum building on New Year's Eve of 1922/23.

Under Rudolf Steiner's consultation Edith Maryon created the eurythmy figures out of ply wood in her determined way and with practical sense. She sawed and painted mainly with her own hands the figures which reminded of expressionistic art. The revenue of the sales was submitted to the Building Fund and later to the Threefold Social Order Association. In his lectures, Rudolf Steiner inserted promotional messages for the figures to buy them.

After World War I, shortage of housing was a problem. To remedy this situation, Edith Maryon initialized on a ground southeast of the Goetheanum building the project "Houses for English People". Rudolf Steiner corrected her drafts and gave complementary suggestions. After the project was finalized, Edith Maryon herself lived there and took care of its administration.

What concerned shape and character of Edith Maryon she was very British. She had red hair, a translucent skin and was rather tall. She was a mediatory hostess for visitors from England and an organizer, and sometimes also a translator for Rudolf Steiner's volumes.[1]

The number of letters Rudolf Steiner exchanged with Marie Steiner von Sivers[2] is approximately comparable with that of Edith Maryon[3].

The fire which burned down the first Goetheanum building could not remain without consequences for the perhaps most important co-worker of Rudolf Steiner. Edith Maryon again fell ill with lung disease and, besides a short time in summer 1923, became so weak that she had to stay in her sickbed. Rudolf Steiner visited her daily when he stayed in Dornach, even during the Christmas Conference 1922/23.

After Edith Maryon's early death at the age of 54, Rudolf Steiner appointed no successor for the Head of the Section Fine Arts.

1 **Steiner, Rudolf:** "Towards Social Renewal: Basic Issues of the Social Question" (CW 23) – Rudolf Steiner Press, 2000. New translation by Matthew Barton.
2 **id. & Marie Steiner von Sivers:** "Correspondence and Documents 1901 - 1925" (CW 262) – SteinerBooks Inc, 1988.
3 **Rudolf Steiner Verlag (ed.):** "Briefwechsel Rudolf Steiner – Edith Maryon: Briefe – Sprüche – Skizzen 1912 - 1924" (GA 263/1) – No English publication available.

Ita Maria Hendrika Wegman

*Physician, Member of the Foundation Board of
the Allgemeine Anthroposophische Gesellschaft
– AAA (General Anthroposophical Society),
Head of the Section "Medicine" of the Freie
Hochschule für Geisteswissenschaft am
Goetheanum (School of Spiritual Science at the
Goetheanum).*

* 12.02.1876 Kravang, Java
  (at that time Netherland's Indies)
† 04.03.1943 Arlesheim (Switzerland)

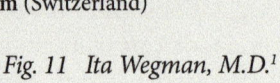

Fig. 11   *Ita Wegman, M.D.*[1]

Ita Wegman was the first anthroposophic physician. Under Rudolf Steiner's initiative and patronage she introduced a new art of healing combining modern natural science with esoteric Christianity. She was born as child of Dutch parents on a sugar plantation in Java's West. Her vita comprised development, study, doctor's office and, in cooperation with Rudolf Steiner, the enhanced anthroposophic medicine. By her cosmopolitical engagement she was able to take over the function of a public representative of Anthroposophy. In 1902 already, at the age of 26, she became a member of the Theosophical Society and soon one of Rudolf Steiner's students. Upon his advice, in 1906 at the age of 30 years, she began her studies in medicine at the Swiss Zürich University where also women had access to the medical faculty.

In 1911 she finished her studies with the Swiss Confederate Medical Diploma which at the same time represents the medical licence in Switzerland. By continuing her professional training as general practitioner and gynaecologist, Dr. Ita Wegman was able to open her first own doctor's office in Basel in 1917. When Rudolf Steiner drew her attention to the mistletoe as healing plant for cancer, Ita Wegman realized a first medicament out of

1   Photo Fig. 11 and adapted text by courtesy of: Stiftung Kulturimpuls, Deutsches Stiftungszentrum, Barkhovenallee 1, 45239 Essen, Germany.

apple mistletoe which she had produced by Adolf Hauser, a Zürich doctor of pharmacy. On 1st of July 1917 this new mistletoe medicament was available for injection therapy. In the same month, Ita Wegman treated her first patients with this new medicament. In that way, more than 100 years ago, the anthroposophic oncological mistletoe therapy started.

In June 1921, Ita Wegman opened her hospital in Arlesheim, where Rudolf Steiner, in the few years until his death in 1925, attended the consultations of about 500 patients and advised their treatment together with Ita Wegman. A concept of Occidental-Christian healing art was developed, an integrative medicine comprising natural and spiritual science. In 1925, Ita Wegman and Rudolf Steiner published the treatise "Essentials for the Enhancement of the Art of Healing According to the Knowledge of Spiritual Science"[1]. This volume is an important basis of anthroposophically enhanced medicine and worldwide serves until today as guideline for anthroposophic medical application.

In 1922, Ita Wegman founded in Arlesheim a therapeutical home for mentally retarded children called "Sonnenhof" (Sun Court) which exists until today.

Contemporaries describe Ita Wegman as royal in walk and gesture, with forceful but delicate expressive hands and blue eyes with light and warm radiance. Her speech was frankly with the distinctive Dutch accent; she listened to people to such an intensity that nobody who experienced it could ever forget.

Witnessing under chock the fire which destroyed the Goetheanum building in the night of 1922/23, in Ita Wegman's soul arose pictures from former earth lives. She was certain to fully dedicate her further life to Rudolf Steiner's humanity task. She immediately founded a committee to re-erect the Goetheanum building and asked friends and former patients in the Netherlands, in Germany and England for donation money.

RECOMMENDATIONS FOR FURTHER LITERATURE
Selg, Peter: "I am for going ahead: Ita Wegman's work for the Social Ideals of Anthroposophy" – SteinerBooks Inc; illustr. ed., 2012.
id.: "Spiritual Resistance: Ita Wegman, 1933 - 1935" – SteinerBooks Inc, 2014.
Weirauch, Wolfgang: "Ita Wegman and Anthroposophy: A Conversation with Emanuel Zeylmans" – SteinerBooks Inc, 2012.

1   Steiner, Rudolf & Ita Wegman: "Essentials for the Enhancement of the Art of Healing According to the Knowledge of Spiritual Science" (CW 27) – ASIN: B0913B8G5W, 2021.

Carl Unger belonged to the pioneers of the anthroposophic movement. Being Rudolf Steiner's direct student and co-worker, he wrote
independent articles on the scientific principles of Anthroposophy.
Besides, he was essentially involved with the foundation and development of the Anthroposophical Society. At the age of 26, he met Rudolf
Steiner for the first time on the occasion of a professional journey to
Berlin in February 1904, where he was sustainably impressed by his
lecture. Rudolf Steiner extraordinarily estimated Carl Unger's profound

Carl Theodor Unger
Researcher, factory owner, administrator
of the first Goetheanum building,
lecturer, author.

* **28.03.1878 Bad Cannstatt**
 (Germany)
† **04.01.1929 Nürnberg**
 (Germany)

Fig. 12 Carl Theodor Unger[1]

and prudent cognitive work. In 1908, Carl Unger entered the German
Section of the Theosophical Society. He was requested to lecture about
the present results of work not only on the occasion of the general
assemblies of the Theosophic Society but also during the conferences
given in connection with the performance of the mystery dramas in
Munich in the years from 1910 till 1913. At the first general assembly

---

1   Photo Fig. 12 and adapted text by courtesy of: Stiftung Kulturimpuls, Deutsches Stiftungszentrum,
     Barkhovenallee 1, 45239 Essen, Germany.

of the Anthroposophical Society in January 1914 in Berlin, Carl Unger offered Rudolf Steiner his co-operation for the Dornach building. Rudolf Steiner and Marie Steiner von Sivers nominated Carl Unger as executor of their last will. In case both legators would die at the same time, he was ascribed also the mandate of Rudolf Steiner's literary legacy. With all the means he disposed of, Carl Unger, in 1919, stood up for the distribution of the idea of threefold social order. As of February 1923, Carl Unger was member of the management board (Vorstand) of the re-founded Allgemeine Anthroposophische Gesellschaft – AAG (General Anthroposophical Society). In this function he took part in the Christmas Conference of 1923/24 in Dornach. Thereafter, Carl Unger visited Dornach almost every weekend.

During Rudolf Steiner's last intensive lecture time until September 1924, Carl Unger stayed uninterruptedly in Dornach and took an active part in almost all of the events. After Rudolf Steiner's death on 30th March of 1925, Carl Unger committed himself to a reconsideration of the Anthroposophical Society and the School of Spiritual Science to which young scientists from the Waldorf School were flocking in droves. He vehemently and courageously engaged himself for the assertion of Rudolf Steiner's last will of 1915 which nominated Marie Steiner von Sivers as sole inheritress of the total legacy. Prominent co-workers of the anthroposophic movement were of the opinion that the legacy belonged to the Society.

On 4th January 1929, Carl Unger travelled to Nuremberg in Germany to give his 13th lecture on "What is Anthroposophy?". Shortly before his lecture, he was shot dead by a mentally disturbed man (Wilhelm Krieger) by three bullets. Already in times before that drama, this man wrote offensive letters and threats against Anthroposophy, especially against Carl Unger.

Elisabeth Vreede

Mathematician, Astronomer,
Member of the Foundation Board of the Allgemeine
Anthroposophische Gesellschaft – AAA (General
Anthroposophical Society), Head of the Section
"Mathematical Astronomy" of the Freie Hochschule für
Geisteswissenschaft am Goetheanum (School of Spiritual
Science at the Goetheanum).

* **18.07.1879 Den Haag** (Netherlands)
† **31.08.1943 Ascona** (Switzerland)

Fig. 13   Elisabeth Vreede[1]

Elisabeth Vreede (pronounced "vrəədə") was the second child of a cultivated family that was devoted to Theosophy. Her father was a solicitor, her mother applied herself in welfare.

As a child she was deeply interested in stars and had an extraordinary memory. Based on the books of the astronomer Camille Flammarion[2] she taught herself the French language and discovered her love for astronomical and cosmological questions.

Around 1900 she began to study mathematics, astronomy and philosophy at the Leiden University, where she probably was one of the first female students who attended lectures of these subjects. In addition she learned the Sanskrit language to study mathematics of ancient India.

In 1903, at the age of 24, she first met Rudolf Steiner at the Theosophical Conference in London and was impressed by his personality. In 1904 she participated at the first conference of the Federation of European Sections of the Theosophical Society in Amsterdam and attended Rudolf Steiner's lecture on "Mathematics and Occultism".[3]

---

1   Photo Fig. 13 and adapted text by courtesy of: Stiftung Kulturimpuls, Deutsches Stiftungszentrum, Barkhovenallee 1, 45239 Essen, Germany.
2   **Flammarion, Nicolas Camille** (1842 - 1925): French astronomer and author of popular-scientific scripts as well as president of Société Astronomique de France (SAF), founded by him in 1887.
3   **Steiner, Rudolf**: "Mathematics and Occultism" (CW 35), published in "Philosophy and Anthroposophy" – Rudolf Steiner Press, 1992.

It has been claimed that Elisabeth Vreede graduated with a diploma in astronomy and astrophysics in 1906. From 1910 to 1914 she lived in Berlin, for a while in the same house where Rudolf Steiner lived. There she was at times co-worker in his office and, upon his suggestion, gave many introducing courses and lectures for laypersons regarding mathematics and astronomy. Originally she had come to Berlin for her doctoral thesis. Since her activities were increasingly determined by the tasks in the scope of the anthroposophic movement, her thesis remained unfinished.[1] Until 1914, Elisabeth Vreede often travelled to places where Rudolf Steiner gave his courses of lectures and played small stage roles in the performances of the mystery dramas in Munich. She was the one who typed and copied the text manuscripts which were written by Rudolf Steiner during the nights.

At the age of 34, in April 1914, Elisabeth Vreede moved to Dornach in order to help along with the building of the first Goetheanum, especially with timber carvings.

During the years of World War I, she interrupted her Dornach stay and volunteered in Berlin to care for prisoners of war.

Around 1918, Elisabeth Vreede began to assist Marie Steiner von Sivers to establish the library and archive at the Goetheanum. She bought from her own funds all postscripts of lectures of Rudolf Steiner as soon as these were typed after having been taken in shorthand. In her modest way, Elisabeth Vreede made her knowledge available to help students and persons seeking advice at the Goetheanum. In 1920 she moved to Arlesheim where she had built a house for herself after a model designed by Edith Maryon and Rudolf Steiner (see Chapter 9).

Elisabeth Vreede played an important role when the three weeks meeting on the occasion of the inauguration of the first Goetheanum building had to be organized in autumn of 1920, where she gave two lectures. During the Christmas Conference in 1923/24[2] at the occasion of the newly founded General Anthroposophical Society, Rudolf Steiner proposed her to become member of the Society's managing board. She established the Mathematical-Astronomical Section of the School of Spiritual Science and launched the first "Rundbrief" (circular) which is published until today by every Section.

RECOMMENDATION FOR FURTHER LITERATURE
Selg, Peter: "Elisabeth Vreede: Adversity, Resilience, and Spiritual Science" – SteinerBooks Inc, 2017.

1   In the so-called Memorandum, Elisabeth Vreede is cited as "D.Phil." (See Chapter 10).
2   **Steiner, Rudolf & Marie Steiner von Sivers**: "The Christmas Conference for the Foundation of the General Anthroposophical Society 1923/24" (CW 260) – SteinerBooks Inc, 2020.

Andrej Belyj is regarded as the most known representative of the younger generation of the Russian literary-philosophic trend of symbolism bringing it to a cultural heyday. Belyj was novelist, poet, cultural scientist, philosopher, memoirist, literary critic, brilliant speaker and polemicist.

Boris Nikolajewitsch Bugajeff
Pseudonym: Andrej Belyj
Writer

* **26.10.1880 Moscow** (Russia)
† **08.01.1934 Moscow**
  (at that time Soviet Union)

Fig. 14   Andrej Belyj[1]

He was highly recognized for the publication already of his second book. After his first creative crises in 1904, the mystical poetic picture of Russia becomes his most important literary theme which will fascinate him until the end of his life. In the same year, at the first time he came across a book of Rudolf Steiner: "Christianity as Mystical Fact: And the Mysteries of Antiquity"[2].

His novel "Petersburg" (1913) is regarded to be one of the most important oeuvres of the Russian symbolism and introduced Andrej Belyj as one of the greatest writers of the 20th century.

The father of Boris Bugajeff alias Andrej Belyj was mathematician and for some years dean of the Physical-Mathematic Faculty of Moscow's University. His mother was a good pianist, loved music and literature.

---

1   Photo Fig. 14: https://anthrowiki.at/images/a/a3/Andrej-Belyj.jpg.
2   **Steiner, Rudolf**: "Christianity as Mystical Fact: And the Mysteries of Antiquity" (CW 8) – Anthroposophic Press Inc; 4th revised ed., 1997.

After having finished his studies at the Natural Scientific Department of the Physical-Mathematic Faculty of Moscow's University, Andrey Belyj committed himself completely to literature which he had started already in the age of 16. In 1901 he got acquainted with Theosophy for the first time, without being attached to it.

In 1909 Andrej Belyj made the acquaintance of Assja Turgenieff, his later wife. Both travelled from Brussels, Belgium to Cologne, Germany to attend a lecture of Rudolf Steiner. From then on, Anthroposophy became the main content of Andrej Belyj's life. Soon after, around his age of 30, he became esoteric student of Rudolf Steiner and, together with his wife Assja, he eagerly attended his lectures in various towns, e. g. Munich, Germany; Oslo, Norway; Copenhagen, Netherlands. In 1912 and 1913 they witnessed in Munich the stage performances of the four mystery dramas of Rudolf Steiner

In March of 1914, Andrej Belyj together with his wife moved to Dornach, Switzerland where they assisted to erect the first Goetheanum building. The construction of this spiritual temple by representatives of many nations who participated in World War I, was experienced by Andrej Belyj as the first sign for a future spiritual culture.

In August 1916 he was called up to serve in the Russian army and returned to his native country by Paris and London. In total, he and his wife attended about 400 lectures of Rudolf Steiner. In Russia he was co-founder of the Anthroposophical Society and gave more than 300 lectures in the course of two years.

Before returning to Russia, the personal relationship between Andrej and Assja Belyi became more and more difficult. In order to meet her and clarify this distressing situation, he came to Berlin in 1921. However, this encounter led to the final separation. Before leaving Germany again, Belyj had a last meeting with Rudolf Steiner who gave him a number of advices for his spiritual development, said goodbye by kissing his forehead and blessed him for his further work in Russia.

As the Bolshevik Government denounced Andrey Belyj's literary work as "bourgeois-decadent", he retired into isolation with his second wife and continued to write but without the possibility of publication.[1]

---

1   Adapted text by courtesy of: Stiftung Kulturimpuls, Deutsches Stiftungszentrum, Barkhovenallee 1, 45239 Essen, Germany.

Margarita Wassijewna Woloschin, born Sabschnikowa
Painter

* 31.01.1882 Moscow (Russia)
† 02.11.1973 Stuttgart Stuttgart (Germany)

Fig. 15 Margarita Woloschin[1]

Margarita Woloschin grew up in a very rich and culturally diversly interested extended family of Tsarist Russia. Two brothers of her father founded an international publishing house.

As of her childhood it was clear that she wanted to become a painter; therefore, she received painting lessons before she did her A-levels (attestat o srednem obrazovanii). When, at the age of 21, she showed pictures at an exhibition for the first time, she became famous overnight, got orders, and museums bought her pictures which partially can be seen until today in Moscow, Astrachan, Pensa, Koktebel and other towns.

Fig. 16 Self portrait by Margarita Woloschin (Zürich 1905).[3]

In 1905, at the age of 23, Margarita Woloschin attended with her brother a lecture of Rudolf Steiner and got a first decisive answer to the question after the sense of live. During the following years, she accompanied Rudolf Steiner on many lecture journeys and learned to mediate between Anthroposophy and Russian mentality. She interpreted Rudolf Steiner, translated his scripts[2], delivered oral and written reports to her Moscow friends and contributed to the foundation of the Russian Anthroposophical Society on 20th September 1913.

---

1   Photo Fig. 15 and adapted text by courtesy of: Stiftung Kulturimpuls, Deutsches Stiftungszentrum, Barkhovenallee 1, 45239 Essen, Germany.
2   Russian translation of M. Woloschin e. g. Rudolf Steiner: "Occult Science: An Outline of Esoteric Science" (CW 13), re-edited with new translation: Rudolf Steiner Press, 2013.
3   Photo Fig. 16 by courtesy of: Russian Sawizki Gallery, Pensa, Russia. In the background there is a building that could be the second Goetheanum – 20 years before it was constructed!

Fig. 17   The seven painting motifs of the small cupola of the first Goetheanum building.[1]

When in 1914 in Dornach the construction of the first Goetheanum building began, Margarita Woloschin started to work as carver until Rudolf Steiner asked her to paint two of the seven motifs in the small cupola – the Slavic motif together with Arild Rosenkrantz, the Egyptian motif alone.

In her autobiography she conceded that it took her many years to understand the directions Rudolf Steiner gave to painters in his lectures on colours[2]. To her opinion these lectures belong to the most mysterious things and that it would take a yearlong practice to capture in a new and different way the experience and use of colours.

For the plant colours to paint the two cupolas and the stage curtain of the Goetheanum building, experiments and first trials were carried out under the direction of Rudolf Steiner in a small laboratory in Dornach. All these impulses and practical results were for the benefit of further artistic works and stage pictures, e. g. for the mystery dramas.

In her interesting memoirs, Margarita Woloschin writes about a conversation with Rudolf Steiner. Upon her question concerning the figure of the "Christ as Representative of Mankind Between Lucifer and Ahriman", he answered: «This face of Jesus Christ should not be treated as a dogma – I see it in that manner. (…) In our time, Christ will be sought in all fields, also in painting.»[3]

RECOMMENDATIONS FOR FURTHER LITERATURE
Strebbing, Peter: "Conversations about Painting with Rudolf Steiner: Recollections of Five Pioneers of the New Art Impulse" – Anthroposophic Press Inc, 2009.
Rosenkrantz, Arild (1870 - 1964): Article in English edition of Wikipedia.

1   **Bemmelen, Daniel van** (1899 - 1982): Reconstruction painting. He belonged to the inner circle of people who, under the patronage of Rudolf Steiner, founded the Waldorf pedagogy. His lifelong activities as initiator and teacher of Waldorf Schools in the Netherlands contributed to their strong spread there. – https://sbk. Goetheanum.org/
2   **Steiner, Rudolf:** "Colour" (CW 291), and the supplementary volume "Knowledge of Colours" (CW 291a) – both published by Rudolf Steiner Press, 1998.
3   **Woloschin, Margarita:** "The Green Snake: An Autobiography" – Floris Books, 2010.

After his high school graduation in autumn of 1904 in Bern, Albert Steffen began to study medicine in Lausanne in Switzerland's Canton Valais because his father wanted him to take over his rural doctor's office. But soon Albert Steffen became aware that these studies did not connect him with life but arose a feeling of wasting away his life. He became clearly conscious that he must become a poet in fact as a synthesis of science, art and religion on the basis of great ideas of mankind.

Albert Steffen

Writer, Member of the Foundation Board of the Allgemeine Anthroposophische Gesellschaft – AAA (General Anthroposophical Society), Head of the Section "Schöne Wissenschaften am Goetheanum" (Literary Arts and Humanities) of the Freie Hochschule für Geisteswissenschaft am Goetheanum (School of Spiritual Science at the Goetheanum).

* 10.12.1884 Obermurgenthal,
  Kanton Bern (Switzerland)
† 13.07.1963 Dornach (Switzerland)

Fig. 18   Albert Steffen[1]

---

1   Photo Fig. 18 and adapted text by courtesy of: Stiftung Kulturimpuls, Deutsches Stiftungszentrum, Barkhovenallee 1, 45239 Essen, Germany.

With his father's permission he broke off his study of medicine and registered at the University of Zürich to study arts and humanity. Beginning of October 1906, he finished his first novel "Ott, Alois and Werelsche" (edited by the publisher S. Fischer in June 1907). A few days later he travelled to Berlin, where he wanted to continue his studies. At the end of February 1907, Karl Stockmeyer drew his attention to a lecture of Rudolf Steiner whom Albert Steffen met for the first time.

During the following years he devoted himself to intensively studying Rudolf Steiner's scripts and to meditative training which he had begun already earlier. In 1910, Albert Steffen joined the Theosophical Society and followed Rudolf Steiner 1913 to join him in his newly founded Anthrosposophical Society.

Besides shorter stays in his native Switzerland, which also lead him to the Goetheanum in Dornach, to make himself useful in the carving workshop, Albert Steffen remained in Munich until summer of 1920, which means that he stayed there during all the time of World War I. During this stay he wrote his two first dramas "The Manichaeans" und "The Exodus from Egypt". For the new anthroposophical weekly "Das Goetheanum"[1], Rudolf Steiner designated the 36-year old Albert Steffen as responsible editor. In this function the writer now could also work as essayist for a new culture on the basis of spiritual science; this expanded his field of activity and at the same time improved his living conditions. Albert Steffen was occupied with this work and connected with the Goetheanum in Dornach also externally until his death in 1963.

After Rudolf Steiner's death, Albert Steffen, on the proposal of Friedrich Rittelmeyer[2], was elected Chairman of the Allgemeine Anthroposophische Gesellschaft – AAG (General Anthroposophical Society) at the extraordinary general meeting on Christmas of 1925.

RECOMMENDATION FOR FURTHER LITERATURE
Steffen, Albert: "Meetings with Rudolf Steiner" – Schöne Wissenschaften, Dornach 1961.

1   The weekly "Das Goetheanum" has been founded by Rudolf Steiner in 1921. It is the only anthroposophic organ of the Anthroposophical Society which appears until today regularly.
2   Rittelmeyer, Friedrich (1872 - 1938) was a German theologian, famous preacher, Lutheran pastor in several towns of Germany, anthroposophist, and, in 1922, co-founder of "Die Christengemeinschaft" (The Christian Community).

Born near Moscow in the countryside, Assja Turgenieff grew up in a sheltered way. At the age of twelve she developed an immense thirst for knowledge which, later on, led her to frequent anti-religious meetings. She experienced street fightings in Moscow of the First Russian Revolution in 1905. Her concerned parents sent her to Paris together with her sister Natascha. Assja Turgenieff's zest for artistic action was awakened by the gorgeous art works in the Louvre Museum. In Paris and soon after in Brussels she made the acquaintance of the engraver and typograph Frédérique Danse who instructed her in drawing and etching art.

At the age of 18, she met Andrej Bugajeff, alias Belyj. As soon as she had finished her training, the couple married and undertook journeys to Sicily, Egypt, Palestine and Greece to come to know of old cultures and their art.

At the age of 22, Assja Turgenieff-Bugajeff met Rudolf Steiner in Cologne, Germany and, thereafter, she and Andrej Belyj travelled with him to attend his numerous lectures in Germany and abroad.

In spring of 1914 Assja and Andrej moved to Dornach to help with the construction of the first Goetheanum building. Assja's sister Natascha Pozzo also joined them. Though Assja was originally designated to grind the glass windows, she began to cooperate with construction drawings and, together with her husband, was scheduled to carve the architraves.

The coloured glass windows of the Goetheanum building were produced in the Glass House. Assja Turgenieff-Bugajeff worked under the directions of the Polish painter and anthroposophist Tadeusz Rychter (c. 1873 in Lviv, Ukraine - c. 1943 in Warsaw, Poland). As time went by, Assja also carved on the timber sculpture "Christ as Representative of Mankind Between Lucifer and Ahriman" under Edith Maryon's supervision. Simultaneously she was engaged to learn eurythmy.

As a consequence of excessive labour, Assja Turgenieff-Bugajeff suffered a health crisis in the winter of 1916/17, forbidding her for a while to go on with carving and eurythmy. To use the time, she pursued the black and white drawings and, together with Rudolf Steiner, developed a new hatching technique. After her recovery, Rudolf Steiner assigned her to etch the window motifs of the first Goetheanum building.

Under the leadership of Marie Steiner von Sivers, Assja performed on stage and on tour with the eurythmy ensemble from 1915 till 1935.

Assja Anna Turgenieff-Bugajeff
Graphic designer, glass grinder, eurythmist.

* 12.05.1890 Moscow (Russia)
† 16.10.1966 Arlesheim (Switzerland)

Fig. 19   Assja Turgenieff-Bugajeff[1]

After the Goetheanum building was burned down, Assja Turgenieff-Bugajeff began the major task to re-design all glass windows of the first Goetheanum for the second building with its high narrow form. The motifs which originally adjoined each other got a vertical order. Only the red window – today in the west of the second Goetheanum building – could be performed in its original form.

The transparency of Assja's being encountered here with the corresponding material: the glass! Physically glass grinding was hard work. The motifs had to be elaborated from the huge glass surfaces by continuous inflow of water. Only after the end of World War II (in 1945) the last windows could be finalized.

Besides this work, Assja Turgenieff-Bugajeff illustrated fairy tales, legends and books for young people. Marie Steiner von Sivers commissioned her to design all book titles and to transfer Rudolf Steiner's blackboard drawings accordingly. Assja communicated her experiences in lectures and courses in Dornach and Bern. After a longer period of suffering, she died at the age of 76 in Arlesheim.

RECOMMENDATION FOR FURTHER LITERATURE
Turgeniev, Assya: "Reminiscences of Rudolf Steiner and work on the first Goetheanum" – Temple Lodge Publishing, 2003.

1   Photo Fig. 19 and adapted text by courtesy of: Stiftung Kulturimpuls, Deutsches Stiftungszentrum, Barkhovenallee 1, 45239 Essen, Germany.

Guenther Wachsmuth

Member of the Foundation Board of the Allgemeine Anthroposophische Gesellschaft – AAA (General Anthroposophical Society), Head of the Section "Science" at the Goetheanum's Freie Hochschule für Geisteswissenschaft (School of Scientific Science).

* 04.10.1893 **Dresden** (Germany)
† 02.03.1963 **Dornach** (Switzerland)

Fig. 20   Guenther Wachsmuth, J.D.[1]

Guenther Wachsmuth was born as second son of a pediatrician and a mother who loved everything that was progressive. At the age of seven, his father suddenly died und awoke him from a childhood dream having lived in a wealthy and bourgeois milieu of the 19th century. He spent longer holiday times at the estate Ussmannsdorf where – together with his brother and sister – he could let off steam freely; the children helped with the harvest, supported during birth of young animals, learned horse riding and hunting. In a cultural landscape they were part of a sound and traditional community life consisting of men, animals and plants.

Since the father's early death, the children were educated by their mother alone. Enthusiastic of everything new, she treated her children in the most progressive ways known in education and health at that time. Simultaneously, she promoted an excellent education and open-mindedness. In autumn of 1912, Guenther Wachsmuth passed the German High School exam (Abitur) in Langensalza. After he had undertaken a journey to Egypt with his mother, he studied law in Oxford for two semesters. His mother married anew and moved to Munich where Guenther Wachsmuth continued his studies in 1914/15.

When World War I broke out in August 1914, Guenther Wachsmuth presented himself as war volunteer. On a patrol ride in Russia, a sabre cut of a Cossack hurt his left arm in such a way that it never again was fully mobile.

---

1   Photo Fig. 20 and adapted text by courtesy of: Stiftung Kulturimpuls, Deutsches Stiftungszentrum, Barkhovenallee 1, 45239 Essen, Germany.

As commissioned officer he discovered his abilities to cope with difficult organisational tasks. After the war, he continued his studies in Munich and completed in 1919 with the Doctorate in Law in Würzburg.

His much esteemed mother had entered the German Section of the Theosophical Society and, in 1912/13 followed Rudolf Steiner in the Anthroposophical Society. On Christmas 1919 she arranged a meeting between Rudolf Steiner and her 26-year-old son Guenther, that ignited his total enthusiasm for Anthroposophy.

In April of 1921, Guenther Wachsmuth moved to Dornach and – together with Ehrenfried Pfeiffer – founded the Research Laboratory in the cellar rooms of the Glass-House which had been erected in 1914 close to the first Goetheanum building. One year later, Rudolf Steiner entrusted Wachsmuth and Pfeiffer with experiments for agricultural preparations.

The destruction by fire of the first Goetheanum building brought about that Guenther Wachsmuth got closer to Rudolf Steiner, becoming his personal assistant, so to speak. He provided him with literature, organized his travels and accompanied him, prudently took care for his protection and, in 1923, he actively engaged himself for the reconstruction of the Goetheanum building. Rudolf Steiner esteemed Guenther Wachsmuth's abilities and energy. On the occasion of the re-foundation of the Allgemeine Anthroposophische Gesellschaft – AAG (General Anthroposophical Society) in 1923/24, he proposed the now 30-year old man as member of the managing board, treasurer and secretary.

As of Christmas 1923, Guenther Wachsmuth committed himself to the complex tasks within the Society. After Rudolf Steiner's death in March 1925, the construction of the second Goetheanum building could be finalized by his dedication. And the Society could be maintained during the difficult times of intern confrontations and World War II. Moreover, he was Head of the Scientific Section and energetically was engaged for the development of biodynamic agriculture and its connection with the School of Spiritual Science.

Besides his organizational performances, especially his conception of the relationship between spiritual and natural science is characteristic for his anthroposophic work. Guenther Wachsmuth fulfilled the tasks he was entrusted with by absolute commitment, organizational skill and "never say die" initiative power.

By his sophisticated multilingualism and his enthusiasm for Rudolf Steiner's social reforms, George Adams became as a young man a marvellous translator of lectures, that Rudolf Steiner delivered in England. He contributed pioneering research results for the anthroposophically extended science of nature on the basis of his studies of theoretical physics, chemistry and projective geometry.

George Adams' Australian father with German roots was a pioneer of the oil industry. His mother was born in England with the family name "Adams" which he adopted in 1940. Shortly after George Adams' birth, the family moved to Solotwina near Stanislawow in the foothills of the Carpathian Mountains. At the age of three, his parents separated and his mother returned to England. It was only in the 1930s that

George Adams Kaufmann
Mathematician, English translator and interpreter of anthroposophic contents, member of the London Emerson Group of the Anthroposophical Society.

* 08.02.1894 Maryampol, East Galicia
   (at that time Austria-Hungary)
† 30.03.1963 Edgbaston near
   Birmingham (England)

Fig. 21   George Adams Kaufmann[1]

---

1   Photo Fig. 21 and adapted text by courtesy of: Stiftung Kulturimpuls, Deutsches Stiftungszentrum, Barkhovenallee 1, 45239 Essen, Germany.

George Adams saw her again, shortly before she died. The timid and melancholic child grew up multilingually, especially with English, German and Polish. The education was organized by English governesses and a young German woman at his father's side who enabled George and his siblings also to experience an intensive life in nature.

As of 1905, George Adams lived in a boarding school in England and travelled alone to Galicia to visit his family in all longer holidays. In 1915 he finished his studies in chemistry at Christ College in Cambridge with an excellent degree.

Around the year 1914 he became acquainted with Rudolf Steiner's occult science and entered the London Emerson Group of the Anthroposophical Society.

In 1920 George Adams married Mary Fox. In the same year he took part in the inauguration of the first Goetheanum. Thereafter he was invited to be Rudolf Steiner's direct interpreter in free speech for the English language and translation of numerous discussions and about 110 lectures. Later on, often together with his wife, he was engaged with many translations of Rudolf Steiner's volumes. Rudolf Steiner appreciated always with warm words George Adams' engagement and talent to translate his extemporaneous lectures of at least one hour by subdividing them in three parts and to present a perfect English translation to the audience only on the basis of some notes. He described this mission as "big sacrifice" for George Adams.

«The task of translating books, scripts and lectures of Rudolf Steiner into another language will still occupy some more generations. (…) Today (1951) Anthroposophy is a substance of active life of people over the whole world. All the way to Honolulu in the west, down to South Africa, Australia and New Zealand in the east there are groups that stand up for Rudolf Steiner's life and work. Also in this year, spiritual science makes good progress.»[1]

RECOMMENDATION FOR FURTHER LITERATURE
Whicher, Olive Mary: "George Adams. Interpreter of Rudolf Steiner: his life and a selection of his essays" – Henry Goulden, 1977.

1   Wachsmuth, Guenther: "The Life and Work of Rudolf Steiner" – SteinerBooks, 1995.

Ehrenfried Pfeiffer was born the same day on which the Kali Yuga ended – the 5,000-year-long era of spiritual darkness: the 19th February 1899.

At the age of five, his father died and his mother moved to Nuremberg where Ehrenfried mainly grew up with the maternal grandparents.

His mother joined the anthroposophic circle of Rudolf Steiner, attended his lectures and – together with her second husband, the anthroposophist Theodor Binder – established an own branch. Rudolf Steiner now and then visited the parents' house. Once Ehrenfried fell seriously ill and Rudolf Steiner's medical advices resulted in his healing. He also gave Ehrenfried a child's prayer which helped him to overcome his fear of surroundings. Rudolf Steiner insistently advised Ehrenfried's mother to never speak to him about Anthroposophy and to not influence him in this direction at all. The boy should find his spiritual way all alone.

At the age of 13, Ehrenfried Pfeiffer belonged to the confirmands in the class of the Lutheran pastor Friedrich Rittelmeyer (see footnote 2, page 47). He taught him the appreciation of true humanity. When Ehrenfried's mother moved with his stepfather to Stuttgart in 1913, he stayed in Nuremberg. His grandfather, pharmacist by profession, imparted to his young grandson his distinctive love for nature as well as an interest in healing substances, and demonstrated to him chemical experiments. Because of Ehrenfried's extreme nearsightedness he early became familiar with loneliness. Therefore, he roamed through nature, observed landscape, river, plants, animals and made the acquaintance of elementary beings. Later on, he once said: «These impulses shaped my whole life and career of research life in such a rich way.»

His strong mental connection to music in connection with an absolute pitch seemed to suggest that Ehrenfried Pfeiffer once would become a musician. However, despite great musical talent (he played the piano and the violin) he failed at the conservatory. Thus, music remained a field of unfulfilled longing throughout his life.

After World War I, he studied electrical engineering and technical physics at the Technical University of Stuttgart. Independent of his parents, Ehrenfried Pfeiffer found access to Rudolf Steiner's work by Carl Unger.

Ehrenfried Pfeiffer
Chemist, Researcher (method of crystallization, quality of food, dynamic agriculture), inventor, lecturer.

* 19.02.1899 München (Germany)
† 30.11.1961 Spring Valley, NY (USA)

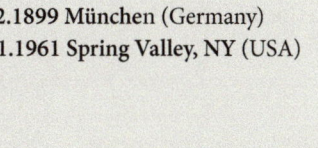

Fig. 22   Ehrenfried Pfeiffer[1]

In 1919, Rudolf Steiner charged Theodor Binder with the financial organisation of the construction management of the Goetheanum building. Thus, Ehrenfried Pfeiffer for the first time came to Dornach. By reason of his experiences as working and technology student, Rudolf Steiner assigned him with the conception and execution of the stage lighting as well as the air condition for the first Goetheanum building. In his English autobiography[2] Ehrenfried wrote in German: «I knew here is my hometown. What lived in me as dreamy spiritual world throughout my youth, what were my ideals and my striving for their manifestation in the physical and rough so-called reality of earth life – all that found its homestead in this place. I had arrived on earth and awoke. I was two months before my 21st birthday.»

From 1920 till 1925, Ehrenfried Pfeiffer took up studies at the Basel University in mineralogy, physical chemistry (on the advice of Rudolf Steiner), botanic, plant geography, ecology, trade history and science as well as psychology. It was an incredible balancing act which he managed between his work at the Goetheanum building and his studies.

---

1   Photo and adapted text by courtesy of: Stiftung Kulturimpuls, Deutsches Stiftungszentrum, Barkhovenallee 1, 45239 Essen, Germany.
2   **Pfeiffer, Ehrenfried**: "A Modern Quest for the Spirit" – Mercury Press, 2010. Treatise on etheric research and nutrition, the etherization of the blood, the function of the heart, and letters from his estate.

Chapter 4

Eurythmy a New Art of Movement

Art is a revelation of secret laws of nature.
Without its active realization it could never become obvious.

Johann Wolfgang von Goethe (1749 - 1832)

Fig. 23   Eurythmic expression for the letter "A".
These three paintings derive from a drawing map of Angelika D.
Albrecht (c. 1995).

The origins of eurythmy derive from Rudolf Steiner's inspirations of the spiritual world which led him also to the knowledge that its secret is hidden in the transfer of the movement of the larynx and its neighbouring organs to the inner rules of the human body in its consecutive movements to mutely express a musical or speech element. Thus, the whole human body becomes a moving larynx. Furthermore, Rudolf Steiner lectured on 12ᵗʰ January 1920: «Eurythmy is also born out of what Anthroposophy is represented with the Goetheanum by Goethe's supernatural conception of the sensual world, nature and art.»[1]

Fig. 24 Eurythmic expression for the mood "Loveliness".

Fig. 25 Eurythmic expression for the mood "Minor".

1 **Steiner, Rudolf**: "An Introduction to Eurythmy" (CW 277 - CW 277a), SteinerBooks 1983 – contains 16 talks preceding eurythmy performances of this 618-page volume.

As of 1908, Rudolf Steiner developed a new anthroposophical art of movement which was named "eurythmy" on 27th September of 1912 during a movement course which Marie Steiner von Sivers gave for her student Lory Smits in the Swiss Bottmingen. Eurythmy metamorphizes speech and vocal organs to a vivid movement of the whole human body in a certain space. The extensive repertoire of eurythmy's means of presentation finally becomes accessible from the anthroposophic ideology alone. «In those early times, Rudolf Steiner drew all the forms that the artists had to create for presenting works of music or literature; often he personally gave examples. Many of these sketches and drawings of Rudolf Steiner are still available and serve the exercising artists until today for training and performance.»[1] Later on, the pure stage art and light eurythmy was joined by special disciplines like pedagogical eurythmy in Waldorf schools and therapeutical eurythmy in medicine.

In her preface to Rudolf Steiner's "Eurythmy as Visible Speech"[2] – a course of 15 lectures given by Rudolf Steiner in response to requests – Marie Steiner von Sivers wrote: «This course represented for Rudolf Steiner one of his favorite children. From small beginnings, it developed quite organically. Like a plant grows shoot by shoot it developed to a strong trunk thanks to its own sound live abundance and the enthusiasm of its representatives. It refined those who were devoted to it and obliged him/her more and more to take off the personal conduct; there was no space for arbitrary behaviour. (…) Now it became possible to present transcendental and subconscious forces into earth life. This enabled us to perform almost all corresponding scenes of Goethe's 'Faust' on the stage of the carpenter's workshop in the Goetheanum building.»

The focus of "Eurythmy as Visible Singing"[3] is the source of movement and gesture in the human being. Movement in musical experience is thus traced back to its origin in the human instrument itself. In these eight lectures, like the degrees of the musical scale, Rudolf Steiner led through eight stages, focusing on the living principles of discovery and renewal as source of movement and gesture in the human being.

1   Wachsmuth, Guenther: "The Life and Work of Rudolf Steiner" – SteinerBooks, 1995 (German edition p. 218).
2   Steiner, Rudolf: "Eurythmy as Visible Speech" (CW 279) – Rudolf Steiner Press, 2020.
3   id.: "Eurythmy as Visible Singing" (CW 278) – Rudolf Steiner Press, 2020.

The means of eurythmic expressions are forms and gestures to which belong five vowels, 15 consonants and 15 moods including major and minor in order to express the recited text (poems, sonnets, verses, quotes etc.). In an introductory speech to a eurythmic stage performance with German, English and French texts, Rudolf Steiner explained, that eurythmy is suited for every language, because it is adapted to the tone. (...) Eurythmy expresses the different language characters in the way how this moved, mute but visible speech is handled.[1] It is not astonishing that pupils in Waldorf schools like to eurythmize their names.

«The art of eurythmy strives to make the invisible visible in a harmonious and disciplined play of colour, form, sound, and motion. During the early years of the twentieth century when eurythmy was young and little known, Rudolf Steiner's introductory speeches prepared nearly 300 audiences for their encounters with this completely new way of presenting drama, poetry, and music through movements of the human body. Full of life and creativity, these lectures represent an introduction to the aesthetic, pedagogical, and therapeutic secrets of this developing art.»[2]

When, in 1912, the interest of the young Lory Maier-Smits brought about Rudolf Steiner's response with fresh creative possibilities, eurythmy was born for the world. This unexpected gift is taught and practiced until today as an art, a subject in schools, enjoyed as a social activity and is applied as a therapy.

Eurythmy usually was musically accompanied by a piano or a string instrument which was adapted to the antique kithara. It was built by the Viennese violin constructor Franz Thomastik (1882 - 1951) based on Rudolf Steiner's ideas. As of 1923, Edmund Pracht (1883 - 1951) accompanied eurythmy at the piano. By deepening and practicing the musical elements, he could make drafts of the first lyre in 1925, according to his own description, without adapting historic models. (See also Chapter 9)

1   **Steiner, Rudolf:** "Eurythmy: The Revelation of the Speaking Soul" (CW 277): Lecture "Expression of the Language Character"– Rudolf Steiner Press, 2020.
2   Quotation: Report Anthroposophic Press Inc.

Among the first composers for eurythmistic stage music was the Danish-Dutch modernist composer Leopold van der Pals (1884 - 1966) and the Dutch Jan Adriaan Stuten (1890 - 1948).

Today eurythmy can be acquired at various institutes worldwide during a five-year vocational training. Stuttgart's Eurythmeum[1] – founded in 1921 by Marie Steiner von Sivers with the assistance of Rudolf Steiner – until today lives in a vivid and always renewing form. Under the direction and artistic geniality of Else Klink (1907 - 1994) this school developed from 1935 till 1991 to the renowned Else-Klink Ensemble with international success.

As of 2006 there exists an official internationally accredited academic chair for eurythmy at the Alanus College in Alfter, Germany.[2]

In his lecture courses of 1920 in Dornach "Mystery of the Universe: The Human Being, Image of Creation"[3] Rudolf Steiner gives interesting hints to eurythmy, e. g.: «…You see, ladies and gentlemen, more audiences of eurythmy performances are used to attend in a more passive way. They remark the lesser articulated leg movement against the more articulated arm and hand movements. To understand this necessitates a commitment of the soul. But in times of cinema, people will not comply with this demand. If you watch a dancing movement where only the legs dance and the arms fulfil some instinctive gestures, you need not think or be compassionate.»

The young men who practised eurythmy in those days, e. g. Edwin Froböse, Fred Poeppig, Ralph and Willy Kux, once asked Rudolf Steiner if it is possible also for the male gender to commit in the new art of movement. He answered: «Of course. For eurythmy is a comprehensive art that is able to ever create new forms of expression by its own character.» At another occasion, Rudolf Steiner annotated: «Eurythmy can be practised from the age of 3 till the age of 90 years.»

1   Eurythmeum Stuttgart – E-mail: info@eurythmeumstuttgart.de – Telefon: 0711 / 236 42 30.
2   The German Alanus College in Alfter was founded in 2002. Actually 400 female and male students get their training by 35 professors. Besides eurythmy, master courses of studies are also offered in pedagogy and art therapy.
3   **Steiner, Rudolf**: "Mystery of the Universe: The Human Being, Image of Creation" (CW 201) – Rudolf Steiner Press, 2001.

Fig. 26   Title of the poster "Study Day to Tone Eurythmy with Lyre. Performed by the Goetheanum Eurythmy Ensemble Festival (16ᵗʰ - 18ᵗʰ of October 2020)".[1]

RECOMMENDATIONS FOR FURTHER LITERATURE
Dubach, Annemarie: "The Basic Principles of Eurythmy" – Mercury Press, 2000.
Siegloch, Magdalena: "How the New Art of Eurythmy Began: Lory Maier-Smits, the First Eurythmist" – Temple Lodge Publishing, 2015.

1   Photo Fig 26: © Peter Stevens, Light Eurythmy Ensemble. – By courtesy of: Thomas Sutter, Director of the Light Eurythmy Ensemble (founded in 2000), Dorfgasse 2, Arlesheim, Switzerland.

In the following are describe short biographies of three eurythmists who closely worked with Rudolf Steiner and Marie Steiner von Sivers from the beginning of eurythmy.

Tatjana Kisseleff first met Rudolf Steiner in 1911/12. At Easter in 1914, Rudolf Steiner invited her to come to Dornach to set up eurythmy at the Goetheanum. As she was kind of reluctant, he pushed her with the following words: «You are the person who can save eurythmy from the threatening soullessness and maintain its true spiritual sacral background.» Until 1927, Tatjana Kisseleff bore full responsibility for everything eurythmistic at the Goetheanum. The audience remembered her as a very special artist.

After the early death of Tatjana's father, her mother moved to St. Petersburg to the grandparents with her two children, were they experienced a happy childhood. Tatjana received a comprehensive education, finishing with a teacher's diploma in French and German. Thereafter, she graduated in technical drawings in order to help her brother with his engineering studies. Incited by her musical talent, she wanted to find a possibility to unfold herself moving in a special musical and rhythmical way of expression. But first her path led her to Lausanne, Paris and Italy to study laws, social sciences and social therapy. When she returned to Russia, she married the painter Nikolai Kisseleff. With him and other like-minded persons she landed innocently in a Tsarist prison. When she became ill, she was quickly released from prison. By lack of other medical advice, Tatjana was sent to a rest cure in the Swiss mountains. At the age of 30, on Christmas 1911, Tatjana Kisseleff encountered Anthroposophy and Rudolf Steiner in Hannover, Germany. In a personal talk, Rudolf Steiner asked her to transmit Anthroposophy to the Russians. Confused at the beginning, she suspected that finally it was that task which she had searched for. After a short introduction in eurythmy during the Munich Festival 1912 and 1913, when this new art of movement was presented on stage for the first time, and by enhancing her knowledge with Lory Maier-Smits in Düsseldorf, Marie Steiner von Sivers sent Tatjana Kisseleff to Berlin to teach eurythmy. But soon she was asked to come to Dornach.

She immediately started as a teacher of eurythmy for grown-ups and children. At the same time, Rudolf Steiner and Marie Steiner von Sivers gave her eurythmy lessons almost daily over many weeks, and Tatjana

Tatjana Kisseleff (born Powalischin)
Eurythmist

* 15.03.1881 Warsaw (at that time Russia)
† 19.07.1970 Dornach (Switzerland)

Fig. 27   Tatjana Kisseleff[1]

Kisseleff matured to a unique performer. Whether she staged spiritual, dramatical or comedic parts, she always astonished and delighted the audience. Under Tatjana Kisseleff's direction, the first public performance took place in February 1919 in Zürich. Thereafter, the young eurythmy group toured Europe for many guest performances. Besides recognition, enthusiasm and gratefulness, the artists had to accept many challenges, hate and offensiveness.

At Easter in 1924, on the suggestion of Rudolf Steiner, Tatjana Kisseleff opened the first school of eurythmy in Dornach. Until today the "Eurythmeum CH"[2] belongs to the compound of eurythmy vocational training within the Section "Redende und musizierende Künste" (Arts of Eurythmy, Speech, Drama and Music) at the Goetheanum leading the students to a bachelor-similar degree in eurythmy with further connection to internationally accepted master courses.

After the death of Rudolf Steiner, Tatjana Kisseleff had to quit her Dornach task in 1927 because her former students and also colleagues wanted to handle eurythmy in a more modern way. When her efforts to establish a eurythmy school for Russian emigrants in Paris failed, Marie Steiner von Sivers called her back to Dornach in 1938. There she indulged in eurythmistic training of actors and assisting Marie Steiner von Sivers to stage Goethe's Faust and other plays. At the request of Marie Steiner von Sivers she wrote her interesting autobiography.[3] In 1949 she was invited to Malsch near Karlsruhe where she worked until her death with children, laymen and eurythmists.

1   Photo Fig. 27 and adapted text by courtesy of:
    Stiftung Kulturimpuls, Deutsches Stiftungszentrum, Barkhovenallee 1, 45239 Essen, Germany.
2   E-mail: info@eurythmie.ch & info@eurythmeum.ch
3   **Kisseleff, Tatjana**: "Eurythmy and Rudolf Steiner: Origins and Development 1912 - 1939" –
    Floris Books, 2021.

**Eleonore (Lory)
Clara Maria Maier-Smits**
Eurythmist

* 06.03.1893 Bochum (Germany)
† 19.09.1971 Laufenburg, Rhine
(Germany)

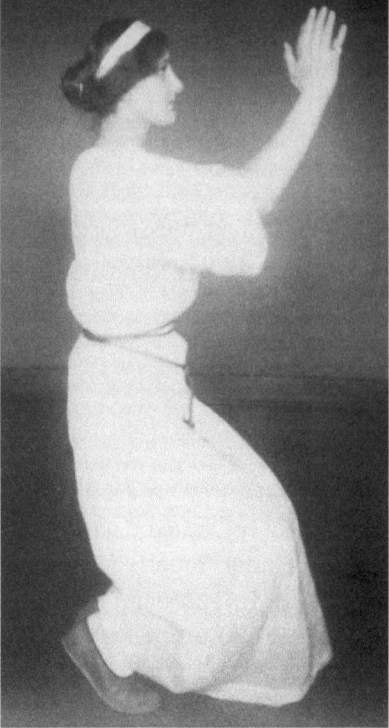

*Fig. 28   Lory Smits, eurythmizing the soul
gesture "I am looking up" (1913).[1]*

Lory Smiths was born in a Theosophy orientated family. Her mother initiated that Rudolf Steiner gave branch lectures in the family's house in
Düsseldorf as of 1904. When Lory was 14 years old, Rudolf Steiner allowed
her to also attend these lectures. In 1911, Lory's father died unexpectedly
because of heart failure. From that time on, her mother strived for the
education of her six children alone. Being enthusiastic about movement,
Lory Smits looked for an appropriate profession. Her mother asked Rudolf
Steiner and he was gladly ready to introduce Lory into an art of movement which was based on Anthroposophy.

In September 1912, Rudolf Steiner gave her the first instructions in
nine training lessons on how to move to the spoken word. Thereafter she
intensively committed herself to elaborate alone and with full responsibility

---

1   Photo Fig. 28 and adapted text by courtesy of: Stiftung Kulturimpuls,
    Deutsches Stiftungszentrum, Barkhovenallee 1, 45239 Essen, Germany.

*Formation drawing for five eurythmists,
attributed to Rudolf Steiner.*

the new art of movement and to make it known in the Anthrosophical Society by stage performances, courses of orientation and training. When World War I broke out in 1914, the 21-year old Lory Smits continued to give this young art a basis on which it could continue to exist and be further developed by Rudolf Steiner. In 1913, Rudolf Steiner invited her to take part in the Summer Festival of the Theosophical Society in Munich. With exhilaration and convincing in talent and variability, Lory Smits presented the eurythmic rehearsal of the Chorus of Gnomes and Sylphs making eurythmy known to a broader audience.

Lory Smits travelled from Munich directly to Stuttgart and other places giving eurythmy courses and performing on stage in Cologne and Berlin. When she came home again after a four-week stay in London, she had big plans. But the beginning of World War I nullified them. Other eurythmists, too, had to experience restrictions. In this situation, Marie Steiner von Sivers decided to take responsibility for the maintenance and advancement of this young art in giving comprehensive eurythmy lessons. Lory Smits married Alfred Maier in May 1917.

In March 1918, Marie Steiner von Sivers asked Lory Maier-Smits to come to Berlin for stage performances. When she arrived there with the news that she was pregnant, Rudolf Steiner advised her to refrain from any kind of eurythmic movements. She returned to Stuttgart, where her first daughter was born.

On the occasion of Rudolf Steiner's great mission to spread the idea of the spiritual-scientific treatment of social and pedagogical questions in Stuttgart from April till July 1919, Marie Steiner von Sivers arranged the first public appearance of eurythmy in Germany. Lory Maier-Smits enjoyed taking part in five great stage performances which accompanied Rudolf Steiner's 17 lectures on the threefold social organism.[1] In August 1920 her second daughter was born.

1   Steiner, Rudolf: "The Renewal of the Social Organism" (CW 24) – SteinerBooks, 1985.

Ilona Schubert belonged to the first formative eurythmists of the Goetheanum stage. With sunny enthusiasm she was fond of everything that had to do with Anthroposophy and art.

Soon after her birth her mother of Hungarian origin died. Her Dutch father was bank director and some time later married a sculptress who became Ilonas' second mother. The uppermiddle-class house of the Bögel family was centre of social events of high cultural level. A connection to Rudolf Steiner was given by the local anthroposophical branch.

From early childhood, Ilona Bögel developed a love for music and liked to move herself. Beginning at the age of five she received dancing education.

In the boarding school of Weimar, Ilona got excited about Johann Wolfgang von Goethe's work what she also expressed in letters home. When her mother showed to Rudolf Steiner one of these letters, he sent the nearly 18-year old Ilona a membership card of the Anthroposophical Society.

Often she attended lectures of Rudolf Steiner and studied his complete works. When she came to know of eurythmy, she took lessons on eurythmy and continued her musical education. A visit to Dornach together with her mother in 1919 was decisive for Ilona Bögel's further life: Marie Steiner von Sivers succeeded in fascinating Ilona for eurythmy in such a way that she stayed in Dornach and immediately began with courses. Rudolf Steiner drew her some eurythmy forms, e. g. the "Butterfly" with a music of Edward Grieg as well as some poems of the young Johann Wolfgang von Goethe. Besides, Ilona Bögel tailored upon Rudolf Steiner's instructions – together with her mother and Helene Röchling[1] – the very first cassocks for the new community for religious renewal "Die Christengemeinschaft" in 1922.

In 1923, Ilona Bögel married the Count Joseph Polzer. The baptism of their son Christward Johannes (a name given by Rudolf Steiner) was the first one of this new Christian community. Because of the Earl's illness, the marriage was soon divorced. Five years later Ilona united with Günter Schubert, a teacher and speaker at the Goetheanum.

---

1   **Röchling, Helene** (1866 - 1945) came across Anthroposophy in 1907, practised eurythmy and was a friend of Rudolf and Marie Steiner. She lived in Mannheim and was married to a partner of the steel mills Röchling Brothers. She founded the Anthroposophic Section II in Mannheim.

Ilona Schubert-Polzer,
(geb. Bögel)
Eurythmist

* 28.03.1900 Mannheim
  (Germany)
† 26.20.1983 Arlesheim
  (Switzerland)

Fig. 29 Ilona Bögel[1], as Bim in "Bim, Bam, Bum" eurythmyzing a poem by Christian Morgenstern[2] (1871 - 1914).

After Rudolf Steiner's death, Ilona Schubert gave eurythmy courses for laypersons but also for expert colleagues and different professional groups. In her autobiography she vividly describes her eurythmistic life. In 1955, she was co-initiator of the "Summer Conference" in Zürich, a free forum of anthroposophic spiritual science. In the first decades students and disciples of Rudolf Steiner and Marie Steiner von Sivers often were under the performers. This conference takes place every year until today.

Among numerous other eurythmists performing during the first time are also the following five: Annemarie Dubach-Donath (1895 - 1973), Alice Margareta Fels-Linke (1884 - 1973), Ralph Kux (1903 - 1965), Willi Kux (1902 - 1976), Fred Poeppig (also actor) (1900 - 1974).

---

1   Photo Fig. 29 and adapted text by courtesy of: Stiftung Kulturimpuls, Deutsches Stiftungszentrum, Barkhovenallee 1, 45239 Essen, Germany.
2   Christian Morgenstern was a member of the General Anthroposophical Society. Rudolf Steiner called him "a true representative of Anthroposophy". Morgenstern's poems have been set to music by numerous composers. His best known works are "The Gallows Songs: Christian Morgenstern's Galgenlieder: A Selection" – University of California Press, 1966.

Chapter 5

UNDER RUDOLF STEINER'S PATRONAGE

If you want to know yourself
Look into the world to all sides.
If you want to know the world
Look into all your own depths.[1]

Rudolf Steiner (1861 - 1925)

Some of the young persons around Rudolf Steiner had an anthroposophic background by their parental home. Most of them were made aware of him by friends or incidentally, as listeners of his lectures and readers of his literature. Then – thunderstruck – they became ardent followers of his spiritual science and soon also members of the Anthroposophical Society.

Most people whose life journey had brought them to Dornach were between 20 and 30 years old and thus lived between their fourth and fifth seven-year life cycle. This means that the influence of the planets has almost past and they could get no forces anymore from the cosmos for their development. At that time, the conscious soul has to handle by itself what it has adopted so far and, therefore, can properly unfold its independent ego.

Partially under extreme physical exertions these young people took part in the erection of the first Goetheanum building. Some remained permanently in Dornach, Basel or Arlesheim, others returned for study purposes or short stays. They all loved their "Doctor" and were at his side to prevent accidents. Many were also at his side in his most difficult period, when he was forced to stay in his sickbed for six months. They had to experience the pain to lose Rudolf Steiner much too early, at the age of 64 years.

In his lifetime, Rudolf Steiner provided his students with ideas and advices for their life plans, the anthroposophic spiritual science and the

---

1   **Steiner, Rudolf** (1923): "Harmony of the Creative Word" (CW 230) – Rudolf Steiner Press, 2001.

erection of the first Goetheanum building. Some of his students got married among each other, and Rudolf Steiner appeared as guardian of their newborns and later as expert consultant concerning their education. Once he changed a baby's nappy because he felt that he or she was too cold in the cradle.

Another time he regretted not having been consulted during pregnancy in order to give helpful advice also in this state.

These young families most of all loved Rudolf Steiner's reintroduction of annual festivals. In nine lectures he spoke of the character of Easter, St. John's, Michaelmas, and Christmas. The following text derives from this course[1]:

«The cleansing power of Michael has to unite with the breathing of the earth to defeat evil. Then Christmas can be celebrated in the soulful earth with the birth of Christ's impulse which continues to mature until Easter. (…) After Christ's resurrection he has connected with mankind and now lives not only in extraterrestrial heights but also within the life of earth. (…) Archangel Michael is the forerunner of a new earth life of the mysteries of birth, entombment and resurrection of Christ.»

Moreover, Rudolf Steiner introduced the assignment of the archangels to the cycles of the year: Archangel Gabriel as the active spiritual character in winter's time, Archangel Raphael in Easter time, Archangel Uriel in summer time and Archangel Michael in autumn time.

In his memoirs, Guenther Wachsmuth describes Rudolf Steiner as follows: «He wanted to be surrounded by free, independent people and, I might say, that on three continents of this earth I have never met a person in whose sphere of life one felt completely free and without restriction whatsoever.»[2]

In his empathetic, attentive and advisory way, Rudolf Steiner provided assistance to everybody. He always warmly greeted by shaking hands and friendly words. He noticed each emotion, took care of personal problems and offered solutions. In case of illness he also gave helpful advices. One of the many of examples is described by Margarita Woloschin in her autobiography:

1   **Steiner, Rudolf:** "The Cycle of the Year: As a Breathing Process of the Earth" (CW 223) – SteinerBooks, 1984.
2   **Wachsmuth, Guenther:** "The Life and Work of Rudolf Steiner" – SteinerBooks 1995.

«One day, Rudolf Steiner noticed that the engineer was distressed. Asked for the cause of his grief he replied that the ophthalmologist had diagnosed cataract of one of his eyes which threatened his other eye to become blind, too. On Rudolf Steiner's question whether he might have had a difficult youth, the engineer affirmed it. Rudolf Steiner answered that this was the cause of his illness, and that he would try to stop the process. He ordered to drink a special tea in certain spaces of time und to meditate an individualized verse. Later on, the engineer had no longer eye problems and – as far as I know – his vision was preserved into old age.»[1]

At another time, Rudolf Steiner called for a doctor at the Arlesheim Clinic and asked him to come and look at the hurt finger of a eurythmist.

On the occasion of the outbreak of World War I, Rudolf Steiner gave lectures for co-workers at the first Goetheanum, the so-called Samaritan Course.[2] In a vivid way he demonstrated the various rescue actions. To stop bleeding when sustaining an injury, he recommended the following meditation verse:

Swell, blood
In swelling work
Active muscle
Stir the germs
Loving care
Heart warming
Be healing breath

Rudolf Steiner's comment: «These lines contain everything needed to care a wound and what can be called the secret of a wound. It is much better than all abstract treatment to have in mind what is effective in the spiritual context of the world.»

At lectures given during World War I, Rudolf Steiner commemorated the soldiers and persons killed in action with an appropriate verse.

The pioneer of Waldorf pedagogy Caroline Heydebrand (1886 - 1938) once complained to Rudolf Steiner about her "roaring class". He advised her to train her weak voice to become more sonorous.

1   **Woloschin, Margarita**: "The Green Snake: An Autobiography" – Floris Books, 2010.
2   **Steiner, Rudolf**: "The Secret of the Wound" – Australian Rudolf Steiner Book Centre, 307 Sussex Street, Sydney NSW 2000. The Centre is quite literally the doorway to Anthroposophy in Australia.

Karl Schubert (1889 - 1949) – one of the first teachers in the Stuttgart Free Waldorf School, who strongly shaped the further development of anthroposophically orientated work with disabled persons – once asked Rudolf Steiner for his advice with a problematic child. He explained how sleepy children have to be awoken in their centre by training their will.

An example how Rudolf Steiner honoured each kind of cooperation of his co-workers with warmest thankfulness demonstrates the following poem dedicated to the patron and donator Helene Röchling.

Holy Night[1]

The soul of earth sleeps
In summer's hot time;
The mirror of sun
Shining brightly
In outer space.

The soul of earth wakes
In winter's cold time;
The true sun
Shining spiritually
In inner being.

Summer's day of joy
Is sleep of earth;
Winter's Holy Night
Is day of earth.

---

1   **Steiner, Rudolf** (1920): "Truth-Wrought-Words: And Other Verses and Prose Passages" (CW 40) – SteinerBooks, 2010.

Chapter 6

THE SECOND GOETHEANUM BUILDING

Loss be benefit for itself.[1]
Rudolf Steiner (1861 - 1925)

Fig. 30   Second Goetheanum – Western frontage with main entrance.[2]

1   **Steiner, Rudolf:** "Twelve Moods: Truth-Wrought-Words: And Other Verses and Prose Passages" (CW 40) – SteinerBooks, 2010.
2   Photo Fig. 30: https://commons.wikimedia.org/wiki/File:Goetheanum_Dornach2.jpg.

In 1925, the construction works began for the second Goetheanum building, which should be erected fully in concrete comprising a volume of 106,000 cubic metres (c. 140.000 cubic yards). That of the first Goetheanum building accounted for 66,000 cubic metres). It was erected from 1925 till 1928. After World War I, it was difficult to procure the necessary material. For example, the Norwegian roof slate with its high amount of Muskovit (mica mineral) was no longer available. The impressive result of the glass plates etching of the first Goetheanum building could not be attained because the special glass was also no longer available. The motifs had been engraved with a carborundum grinder in the plain glass according to a slash method developed by Rudolf Steiner.

In his autobiography Ehrenfried Pfeiffer gives the following atmospheric picture: «It was the strong will of the members of the Anthroposophical Society to erect a new Goetheanum building. They urged Rudolf Steiner to give his advice and to create a new model. In addition to the insurance amount of 3.2 million Swiss Franc which only covered the material value and which would have been more appropriate with a sum of 10 million Swiss Franc, the members collected further money in order to be able to start with the works. However, in those years of economic catastrophe, inflation, nations' reconstruction sufficient donations took years. These economic restrictions had an impact until World War II and brought about that the anthroposophic movement could never substantially recover from the crisis. Because of his occupation to reorganize the Anthroposophical Society, Rudolf Steiner could not finalize the plaster model of the new Goetheanum building. And then eventually his illness precluded him from taking the time for it. The new model remained incomplete just as did the second Goetheanum building for many years.»[1]

1   Pfeiffer, Ehrenfried: "A Modern Quest for the Spirit (1899 - 1961)" – Mercury Press, 2010.
     By courtesy of: Perseus Publishing House (translation from German 3rd edition), Basel 2003 (p. 103).

Fig. 31   Second Goetheanum – South frontage with main entrance.[1]

And Guenther Wachsmuth wrote in his memoirs: »The architects only had Rudolf Steiner's rudimentary drawings of its archetype, which he had made and handed out during the Christmas Conference in 1923/24. With this original and the unfinished model the topping of ceremony could be celebrated two years later. And four years later the mighty building was completed in its outer forms and inner structure in such a way that the 3,000 visitors who came to Dornach in 1928 for its inauguration could dedicate it to its purpose.«[2]

1   Photo Fig. 31: © Free Art License by Wladyslaw 4th May 2008.
2   **Wachsmuth, Guenther**: "The Life and Work of Rudolf Steiner" – SteinerBooks, 1995.

Chapter 7

NINE MONTHS OF HIGHEST ACTIVITIES

Knowing is not enough; we must apply.
Willing is not enough; we must do.
Johann Wolfgang von Goethe (1749 - 1832)

After having resumed his activities for lectures and journeys after the first Goetheanum building had been burned down, Rudolf Steiner mastered a number of mere superhuman tasks as of January 1924, which brought him to his physical limits and finally to his sickbed nine months later.

- In Dornach, from 2nd till 9th January 1924, Rudolf Steiner gives his third medical course with eight lectures to young physicians and medical students[1]. The character of this course was completely different from previous presentations. Responding to medical questions it offered unique, groundbreaking insights into the practice and art of healing.

- From 27th February till 24th September 1924, Rudolf Steiner gives 61 lectures to workers of the Goetheanum building. The so-called Workers' Lectures which had already started in August 1922 were neither finalized cycles with a special subject nor announced lectures for a certain audience. Later on, these 113 lectures were collected in eight volumes and represent in the truest sense of the word a "popular" introduction into the research results of Anthroposophy.[2]

---

1   **Steiner, Rudolf:** "Understanding Healing: Meditative Reflections on Deepening Medicine through Spiritual Science" (CW 316) – Rudolf Steiner Press, 2013.
2   **id.:** Workers' Lectures:
    CW 347   "From Crystals to Crocodiles…" – Rudolf Steiner Press, 2004.
    CW 348   "Health and Illness II" – Rudolf Steiner Press, 1981.
    CW 349   "From Limestone to Lucifer…" – Rudolf Steiner Press, 2000.
    CW 350   "Rhythms in Cosmos and Human Beings" – No English publication available.
    CW 351   "Bees" – SteinerBooks, 1998.
    CW 352   "From Elephants to Einstein…" – Rudolf Steiner Press, 2002.
    CW 353   "From Comets to Cocaine…" – Rudolf Steiner Press, 2002.
    CW 354   "From Sunspots to Strawberries…" – Rudolf Steiner Press 1981.

- On 26th of March 1924 Rudolf Steiner travels by car with Guenther Wachsmuth and Ernst Lehrs (Waldorf teacher and accredited lecturer) to Stuttgart's Free Waldorf School, founded five years ago with 200 children and approximately 15 teachers. He opens the monthly celebration with a speech and guides the teachers' conference.

- On the same day, with a night train, Rudolf Steiner travels to Prague to give eleven lectures and to have various conversations during the nine-day Conference of the Czech Anthroposophical Society. At the eurythmy performances directed by Marie Steiner von Sivers, he also gives a speech about the character of eurythmy.

- From 8th till 13th April 1924, Rudolf Steiner is again in Stuttgart's Free Waldorf School which meanwhile is attended by more than 700 pupils in 24 classes. The 1,700 listeners of his five lectures honour him – as one participant describes – «with deeply moving applause at the end of every lecture, while at the end of the last lecture the applause became an ovation that seemed as if it would never end». People had already begun to realize the potential and the promise for the future that Waldorf education held out to the children of the world. Since the establishment of the Waldorf School in 1919, Rudolf Steiner guided it and observed very closely all that what happened. As a result, he was able to excerpt and present the essentials of Waldorf education with elegance as well as with the urgency he felt for the coming times.[1]
In a personal round of talks attended by the teachers, Rudolf Steiner bid farewell to the pupils of the 12th graduating class. The Youth Course scheduled for November in Dornach had to be cancelled because Rudolf Steiner had already retired to his sickbed.
One of these pupils – Karin Ruths-Hoffmann – later related: «Rudolf Steiner had given us a motto for guiding our life to which we listened standing upright. Afterwards we could pick up this saying in written form and he advised us explicitly to meditate it regularly – then we could see what consequences this might arise…»[2]
Together with her classmates she attended Rudolf Steiner's burial in Dornach one year later in April 1925.

1   **Steiner, Rudolf**: "The Essentials of Education: Foundations of Waldorf Education" (CW 308) – Anthroposophic Press Inc, 1996.
2   **Krück von Porturzy, Maria J.** (editor): "Wir erlebten Rudolf Steiner" ("We witnessed Rudolf Steiner") – Verlag Freies Geistesleben, Stuttgart 1956 (p. 209).

• From 13ᵗʰ till 17ᵗʰ April 1924, we find Rudolf Steiner in Bern with five lectures on Waldorf education. «We must develop an art of education that can lead us out of the social chaos into which we have fallen during the last few years and decades. (…) There is no escaping this chaos unless we can find a way to bring spirituality into human souls through education, so that human beings may find a way to progress and to foster mankind's development of civilization out of the spirit itself.»[1]

• Returned to Dornach, Rudolf Steiner takes care of the matter concerning the erection of the second Goetheanum building and – after a personal interview at the Council of Solothurn on 21ˢᵗ of May 1924 – he receives final permission to erect the new building.

• The Easter course for physicians and medical students comprises five lectures in Dornach from 21ˢᵗ till 25ᵗʰ April 1924. »Among plenty of other topics, Rudolf Steiner addresses inflammation and excessive growth; the scarlet fever and measles; the importance of a child's food and breast milk; the functions of the liver, heart, head, and skeleton; the incarnation process; karma as a guide for the physician; morality as a force flowing in from the cosmos; the cosmic trinity of Saturn, Sun, and Moon in healthy and sick people; and the human heart's involvement in thinking.»[2]
One of the young medics – Kurt Magerstädt (1899 bis 1964) – who had also taken part in the speech and drama course and the pastoral medical course and who had taken the state exam in medicine shortly before, summarized his impressions and thoughts of that time as follows: «Each field Rudolf Steiner touched upon became as fresh as a daisy. Every aspect was completely new, there were no repetitions, neither in the wording nor in the train of thoughts. A brimming source blessed us. We drank and did not suspect that we saw our teacher for the last time in his earthly body.»[3]

1   Steiner, Rudolf: "The Roots of Education" (CW 309) – Anthroposophic Press Inc; 3ʳᵈ ed., 1997.
2   id.: "Understanding Healing: Meditative Reflections on Deepening Medicine Through Spiritual Science" (CW 316) – Rudolf Steiner Press; illustr. ed., 2013.
3   Krück von Porturzy, Maria J. (editor): "Wir erlebten Rudolf Steiner" (We witnessed Rudolf Steiner) – Verlag Freies Geistesleben, Stuttgart 1956 (p. 146).

- From the six volume cycle "Karmic Relationships: Esoteric Studies"[1] Rudolf Steiner gives 81 lectures in several towns in Switzerland (Dornach, Zürich, Bern), Czechoslovakia (Prague), France (Paris), Silesia (Breslau), The Netherlands (Arnhem), England (Torquay, London), Germany (Stuttgart). These profoundly esoteric lectures examine the underlying laws inherent in reincarnation and karma, and explore among others the incarnations of specific historical figures.

- During the agricultural course from 7th till 16th June 1924 at the estate of Count Carl Keyseringk in Koberwitz near Breslau, Silesia (today Kobierzyce, a small Polish village near Wrocław), Rudolf Steiner gives eight lectures and numerous hours in answering questions. In a speech on 20th June he quotes: «Today nobody knows that all these mineral fertilizer types just are those that essentially contribute to this degeneration, to this deterioration of agricultural products. For today everybody thinks, that plant growth needs a certain amount of nitrogen – and people do not care about the preparation and origin of this nitrogen. But it does not.» Hundred years ago, Rudolf Steiner initiates in Koberwitz a forward-looking impulse for later consciousness in ecological context: the biodynamic agriculture which still booms in this region. Rudolf Steiner: »Around the mid-twenties century the spiritual scientific knowledge must have become life practice in order to prevent unspeakable harm to the health of nature and man.»
In the afternoon, Rudolf Steiner speaks about karmic relationships in Wrocław; in the evening he gives information on the artistic performances of Marie Steiner von Sivers.
Meetings with youth groups are also part of the program.[2]
During the eleven nights in Koberwitz, Rudolf Steiner continues to write treatises for the monthly publications "Das Goetheanum" and "Nachrichtenblatt für die Mitglieder der Anthroposophischen Gesellschaft" (Information Bulletin for the Members of the Anthroposophical Society)

RECOMMENDATION FOR FURTHER LITERATURE
Paull, John (2011): "Attending the First Organic Agriculture Course: Rudolf Steiner's Agriculture Course at Koberwitz, 1924" (archived 2019-12-29 at the Wayback Machine), European Journal of Social Sciences 21(1).

1   Steiner, Rudolf: "Karmic Relationships: Esoteric Studies" (CW 235 - CW 240) – Rudolf Steiner Press: Vol. I, 2013. Vol. II, reprint ed. 2013. Vol. III: 2013. Vol. IV, 2013. Vol. V reprint ed. 2013. Vol. VI, 1989. Vol. VII, 1973. Vol. VIII, 2nd ed., 2015.
2   id.: "Spiritual Foundations for the renewal of agriculture" (CW 327) – Biodynamic Farming & Gardening Association, 1993.

as well as ritual texts for the Act of Consecration to be spoken by the priests of "Die Christengemeinschaft" until St. John's Festival. After these short nights, Rudolf Steiner hands over to the lady of the house, Mrs. Keyserlingk, every morning a large number of letters to have them sent by post. Most of the largest part of his literary works was written by Rudolf Steiner during the night.

- From 25th June till 7th July 1924, Rudolf Steiner stays at Stuttgart's Free Waldorf School to give the "Curative Education Course" with twelve lectures.[1]

- On 17th of July in 1924, Rudolf Steiner travels to Arnhem, Netherlands to lecture on karma (CW 240) and the anthroposophic movement. After one of these evenings he suffers a fainting spell in his hotel and collapses. He recovers and gives the further lectures as planned.

- On 31st of July 1924, Rudolf Steiner again stands in front of the workers at the Goetheanum in the lecture hall of the carpenter's workshop waiting for their thematic proposals to give extemporized answers.

- Rudolf Steiner's last journey abroad on 11th August 1924 brings him to the International Summer School of the Anthroposophical Society in Torquay, England. The simultaneous translation of his eleven lectures from the cycle "True and False Paths of Spiritual Reseach" and lectures about karma as well as pedagogy is managed as many times before by the mathematician George Adams.[2]
  Rudolf Steiner uses this stay to walk up the hill to visit the remnants of the wall of King Arthur's medieval fortress above a cliff on the lonesome coast of Cornwall Castle. He is accompanied by Guenther Wachsmuth who describes this impressive excursion in his memoirs of Rudolf Steiner[3].
  On 1st of September 1924, Rudolf Steiner returns to Dornach and Marie Steiner von Sivers describes him as being "exhausted".

---

1   **Steiner, Rudolf**: "Education for Special Needs: The Curative Education Course" (CW 317) – Rudolf Steiner Press; 2nd ed., 2015.
2   **id.**: "True and False Paths of Spiritual Research" (CW 243) - Rudolf Steiner Press, 2009.
3   **Wachsmuth, Guenther**: "The Life and Work of Rudolf Steiner" – SteinerBooks, 1995.

From 5th till 22nd September 1924 – three weeks before Rudolf Steiner had to retreat to his sickbed – he gives the following lectures and courses:

- 19 lectures, conversations and answering questions in response to requests from priests of "Die Christengemeinschaft", the movement for religious renewal, which itself had taken form on the basis of Steiner's insights. In front of more than 100 people, Rudolf Steiner speaks about the paths that fertilize religious appearance by spiritual knowledge and about how it can be led into new cultus performances.[1]
Emil Bock (1895 - 1959), priest and "Erzoberlenker" (corresp. Archbishop) of "Die Christengemeinschaft", writes in his treatise "Religious Renewal": «Only time by time I learned what incredible rich and broad foundation of a cosmic-human understanding of Christ Rudolf Steiner had given at this time.»[2]

- Together with Marie Steiner von Sivers, Rudolf Steiner organizes the "Dramatic Course" and gives 19 lectures.[3]

- From 5th till 28th September 1924, Rudolf Steiner gives ten lectures of the karmic cycle and holds his last speech.[4]

- Rudolf Steiner signs the 12,000 member cards thus documenting the importance for him as Chairman of the Anthroposophical Society concerning the personal contact with every single member.

- From 8th till 18th September 1924, Rudolf Steiner gives eleven lectures for about 100 physicians and priests.[5] Albert Steffen quotes Rudolf Steiner as follows: «Christ's way to Golgotha is the highest culmination of medical services. Christ's way further to resurrection is the highest culmination of pastoral services.»[6]

1   Steiner, Rudolf: "The Book of Revelation and the Work of the Priest (CW 346) - Rudolf Steiner Press; illustr. ed., 1999.
2   Krück von Porturzy, Maria J. (editor): "Wir erlebten Rudolf Steiner" (We witnessed Rudolf Steiner) - Verlag Freies Geistesleben, Stuttgart 1956 (p. 146).
3   Steiner, Rudolf: "Speech and Drama" (CW 282) - Anthroposophic Press Inc; illustr. ed., 1960.
4   id.: "Karmic Relationships: Esoteric Studies" (CW 238) - Rudolf Steiner Press, 2009.
5   id.: "Broken Vessels: The Spiritual Structure of Human Frailty" (CW 318) – Anthroposophic Press Inc; revised ed. 2003.
6   Steffen, Albert: "Begegnungen mit Rudolf Steiner" (Encounters with Rudolf Steiner) - Verlag für Schöne Wissenschaften, 5th ed. Dornach, 2009 (p. 349).

With 70 lectures (four till five every day) and the timely completion of the three big cycles (CW 282, CW 342 - 346, CW 318) Rudolf Steiner finishes his activities as lecturer. For the weekly periodical "Das Goetheanum" he submits articles like "The Michael Mystery"[1] and "The Story of My Life 1861 - 1907", his unfinished autobiography.[2]

Upon his sickbed there lay his corrected proof sheets of the work "Fundamentals of Therapy: An Extension of the Art of Healing Through Spiritual Knowledge"[3] which he had begun with Ita Wegman. This volume is destined for physicians and deals with the basic presentation of healing according to the anthroposophic-medical guidelines for physicians throughout the world. The intention is not to underrate the scientific and technological medicine of today, but to illume it beyond its present materialistic outlook with a deeper realization of the nature of the human being.

During his last speech on 27th September 1924, enveloped in his cloak, Rudolf Steiner sits in an armchair in the lecture hall of the carpenter's workshop and closes with the words that are both farewell and appeal:

> *You, the spirit understanding pupil,*
> *Effectively take up Michael's wise waving,*
> *Take up effectively the love-word of world's will*
> *In the high targets of souls.*[4]

Guenther Wachsmuth (1893 - 1963) summarized in his memoirs: «Rarely a person of our time in all countries, groups of men, professions and spheres of acting domains has released so much natural love, worship and at the same time open-mindedness that was simply possible for Rudolf Steiner by his being.»

1   Steiner, Rudolf: "The Michael Mystery" (CW 26) – SteinerBooks, 1984.
2   id.: "The Story of My Life 1861 - 1907" (CW 28) – Anthroposophic Press Inc, 2005.
3   id. & Ita Wegman M.D.: "Fundamentals of Therapy: An Extension of the Art of Healing Through Spiritual Knowledge" (CW 28) – Rudolf Steiner Press (London), 1983.
4   id. (1925): "Truth-Wrought-Words: And Other Verses and Prose Passages" (CW 40) – SteinerBooks, 2010.

Chapter 8

Farewell to Rudolf Steiner

Ex deo nascimur – In Christo morimur – Per spiritum sanctum reviviscimus
From God we are born – In Christ we die – By the Holy Spirit we are reborn

Rosicrucian oath (c. 1616)

Fig. 32   Seal for the first mystery drama[1]

In the course of his numerous lecture journeys to the most different European towns which Rudolf Steiner reached by car, train or ship, he got into life-threatening situations. On 15th May 1922 he lectured in Munich's hotel "Bayerischer Hof". On leaving the podium, right-wing rioters harassed him who had to be put out by the guardians under physical exertion. After this incident (following the incident a dagger was discovered) it was recommended for Rudolf Steiner not to undertake lecture journeys to Germany anymore.

That somebody made direct attempts on Rudolf Steiner's life could only be assumed and nobody believed his corresponding hints. However, what happened on the last day of the Christmas Conference during the afternoon reception on 1st January 1924, really was a poisoning attack on his life. Since Rudolf Steiner forbad to speak of it, only many years later people who were present at this event dared to publish eyewitness reports.

---

1   **Steiner, Rudolf**: Seal for the first mystery drama "The Portal of Initiation" with the initials of the Rosicrucian oath EDN JCM PSSDR. – https://anthrowiki.at/Datei: Mysteriendramensiegel_1.gif.

In 1947, Marie Steiner von Sivers' Italien eurythmy student Lidia Gentilli-Baratto (1903 – 1996) published a booklet (out of print) „Eine Erinnerung an Marie Steiner„ (A Memory of Marie Steiner). It contains the following report of Marie: «Yes, Rudolf Steiner was poisoned the last day of the Christmas Conference at the afternoon reception in the carpenter's workshop. I sat in the hall for a long time while the others, around the 'Doctor' came and went. At a certain moment something terribly incomprehensible seized my soul. I felt to fend off something, and I did not know how and what. At a certain moment I could no longer bear to be seated and went into my backward room. (…) Being in a conversation with Mr. Wachsmuth, suddenly the 'Doctor' came in, green like this leaf. He leaned at the doorpost, desperately looked at us and said: 'We are poisoned'. I was petrified with horror. He immediately asked us if we had drunk something. He breathed a sigh of relief when I denied and nothing has happened to Mr. Wachsmuth. 'So, only I – that's good', he aspired and staggeringly entered the room. Mr. Wachsmuth wanted to immediately call for a doctor but Mr. Steiner forbad it with every emphasis. (…) Then Mr. Steiner ordered to bring him all the milk available. The whole evening and the whole night, he continued to drink milk and saved him by this gastric lavage. (…) Since that day he was doomed to die.»

To what extent the "occult powers" tried to impede the revelations of Rudolf Steiner which they wanted to keep only for their own purposes, describes Guenther Wachsmuth in his memoirs: «Rudolf Steiner removed the invisibility cloak of this secret knowledge, operating in the eastern and western world in an esoteric and exoteric, planned and enigmatic way. (…) He confronted those dark extremes with the central spirit and enlightened the obscure corners. (…) He made aware the fact that the attempts in east and west to let flow spirituality again into the evolution of present time, work with means that are false, power-political and egoistic or at least unsuitable and destructive to higher truths. It is a quite natural and typical phenomenon that by those disclosures of the failures and aberrations these sides confronted him with the most fierce, hateful and passionate hostility. Those who knew what was at stake, at first tried to win him over. As this failed they tried to hush him up. As this also failed, they tried to ridicule him. As this finally also failed, they tried to hamper his work with all means and to possibly destroy this person who stood upright and called things by their real names.»[1]

After having overcome a severe disease, Ehrenfried Pfeiffer returned once again to Arlesheim and Dornach. To an audience of about 30 or 40 people he uttered the wish to entrust them with something before leaving earth in peace. One of the reasons why he emigrated to America in 1940 was the search for encountering real knowledgeable people of the mechanic occultism. Soon he was able to build a confidential relationship with such a person. Speaking with him one day about Rudolf Steiner's different life stages, his conversation partner made the following surprising and dramatic statement: «Please excuse me, but I have to tell you something that might extremely frighten you and that might separate us again which I would regret very much. It was me who was ordered to poison Rudolf Steiner! This poisoning was not intended to kill him but bring him in a position to no longer can confidently control his high occult abilities and consequently eradicate them. Opponents could argue that all his followers would come in such conditions.»[2] Ehrenfried Pfeiffer indicated that Rudolf Steiner had only survived this poison attack with the help of spiritual powers and that the "Brothers of the Left Hand" had not succeeded.

The rumor that Rudolf Steiner has died as a result of this attack 15 months later, was contradicted by Guenther Wachsmuth in his memoirs. Like other people in Rudolf Steiner's next surrounding who were on his side during his last years, first disease symptoms became obvious before and were watched with sorrow. Guenther Wachsmuth writes: «The events of the last years of his life that he endured heroically – e. g. the destruction of the first Goetheanum building or the struggle with enemies and opponents – sapped his physical energy. In addition, his sacrifice to stand at the absolute disposal of a seemingly endless number of members and other people who came to him for personal inquiries or seeking advice was far in excess of normal human dimensions and burden. Rudolf Steiner himself pointed to those facts when, in October 1924, he was forced for the first time to cancel a lecture journey.»[3]

1   Wachsmuth, Guenther: "The Life and Work of Rudolf Steiner" – SteinerBooks, 1995.
2   Pfeiffer, Ehrenfried: "A Modern Quest for the Spirit (1899 - 1961)" – Mercury Press, 2010.
    By courtesy of: Perseus Publishing House (translation from German 3rd edition)
    Basel, 2003 (p. 122 ff.).
3   Wachsmuth, Guenther: "The Life and Work of Rudolf Steiner" – SteinerBooks, 1995.

And Ehrenfried Pfeiffer describes in his autobiography how he walked the way to the studio in the carpenter's workshop on the day of Rudolf Steiner's death:

«In the morning of 30th March of 1925, I went up to the Goetheanum building. The night before, I had a disconserting dream about my beloved teacher. – It was a typical early spring morning with fresh wind, sunshine and clouds that chased each other, and a tender light emitted to pour out above the landscape. – At the door to Rudolf Steiner's studio where he had spent almost six months under the faithful care of his collaborator and physician Ita Wegman, I felt shaking. The door stood open. As Rudolf Steiner had wished, he has died at sunrise. A whole world of activities, hopes for directions to erect the second Goetheanum, to foster the School for Spiritual Science at the Goetheanum and the anthroposophic movement broke down. At that time, only few people were present, e. g. those who cared for the last services, Ita Wegman and two of her assistant physicians. Guenther Wachsmuth and Albert Steffen were already gone. Some guarding men helplessly stood in front of the studio. (…)

For all of us, Rudolf Steiner's death came suddenly. Marie Steiner von Sivers was in Stuttgart and was called back by telephone. I reluctantly entered to see Rudolf Steiner on his deathbed opposite of the statue 'Christ as Representative of Mankind between Lucifer and Ahriman'. I helped to carry out the most necessary things, otherwise speechless and lost. Soon the wake was organized, Rudolf Steiner's corpse prepared for visitors whose line did not come to an end. Thousands of members came from all over the world to pay him their last respect. His face had changed; one could recognize the effects of his suffering. But a divine beauty and freshness remained for several days. This was the face that was shaped by deepest spiritual insight, fierce determination, love, friendliness, and much physical and spiritual suffering. Also a complete foreigner could recognize the great individuality that has used this body. (…) Guenther Wachsmuth, Georg Groot, Edmund Pracht and I were the coffin bearers who fulfilled their duty with broken heart.»[1]

1   Pfeiffer, Ehrenfried: "A Modern Quest for the Spirit (1899 - 1961)" – Mercury Press, 2010. By courtesy of: Perseus Publishing House (translation from German 3rd edition) Basel, 2003 (p. 223/234).

Always, Rudolf Steiner conveyed in his lectures the importance of death in people's life. In his volume "Our Dead …"[1] «we meet Rudolf Steiner in a different way. Here, the substance of what he communicates is less what he says than how he says it; he emphasizes, above all, the tenderness and compassion with which he unites with the souls of the departed in the spiritual world and those grieving on earth. Through his words, heaven and earth, the spiritual and earthly worlds, are brought closer together. Through his example, embodied in his words filled with feeling, a bridge is revealed over which we may cross.»[2]

Rudolf Steiner was present at many funerals of his students, friends or co-workers giving memorial speeches. In case he could not come, he sent consolation letters like the following of 31st December 1905 (the husband of the wife had just died): «If a person dear to us transits in the other world it is especially important that we send him our thoughts and emotions without the wish to have him back. This impedes the deceased his existence in the sphere into which he has to enter. We shall send him not our grief but our love.»[3] Besides, Rudolf Steiner advised bereaved for comfort to connect in gratitude with their dead before falling asleep in prayer or conversation. This could bring solutions for problems upon awakening.

Among the cult rituals that Rudolf Steiner had worked out for "Die Christengemeinschaft" (Christian Community) – e. g. formation, text, robes for the act of consecration, ordination, and sacraments – also a funeral ritual was introduced. With this innovative cultus, the first priest of this new community Rudolf Rittelmeyer took his leave of the deceased Rudolf Steiner.

1 **Steiner, Rudolf**: "Our Dead: Memorial, Funeral, and Cremation Addresses 1906-1924" (CW 261) – SteinerBooks, 2011.
2 Quotation: Report SteinerBooks.
3 **Steiner, Rudolf**: "From the History and Contents of the First Section of the Esoteric School: Letters, Documents, and Lectures: 1904 - 1914" – SteinerBooks, 2010.

In Memoriam of Rudolf Steiner

Let us rise our souls' best thoughts
Up to the spiritual light of the world! –

Where you live with your soul's being,
Where you think in world thoughts' will,
Where you act within the creative stream of time.

Your voice, sounding on earth,
Re-create itself anew from loving heart remembrance
And revive like dew our thoughts of memory.

May us be created in listening silence of world
Your spiritual character in etheric beauty,
Indestructible, like basing in spirit.

May run through us your holy will of creator,
Like you sacrificed it for world aims of mankind
As you actively gifted us while walking on earth.

Let us unite with you in holy flame of sacrifice,
In the deepest centre of our hearts
With the being of your sacrificing gift.

That we see you in death
As the helpful spiritual guide!

Fred Poeppig (27.2.1940)[1]

---

1 Fred Poeppig (1900 - 1974) was an actor, a eurythmist, and a close associate of Rudolf Steiner.

Chapter 9

WAYS OF LIFE AND SITES OF ACTIVITIES AFTER RUDOLF STEINER'S DEATH

Like a man, when day is grey, forgets the sun,
Though it shines and sparkles incessantly,
One may forget you on grey days,
To feel again and again
Shakened, even dazzled,
How inexhaustibly on and on and on
Your sun spirit
Shines for us, the dark wanderers.[1]

Christian Morgenstern (1871 - 1914)

In her autobiography, Margarita Woloschin compares the fate of every man or woman who experienced Rudolf Steiner with that of Parsifal: «He must seek what happened to him. The tasks Rudolf Steiner had left behind in all fields are as big as man's longing for spirituality. For myself personally, I can say that the conscious work has only begun after the death of my teacher. The riper somebody becomes the richer becomes life within and around him or her. I also feel secure in the community. Through all inner and outer obstacles shine, though weakly, those seeds that have the power to save the idea of man.»[2]

The following examples may show in what way the seeds of Rudolf Steiner bore fruits until today.

---

1   **Morgenstern, Christian:** Tribute to Rudolf Steiner after his death.
2   **Woloschin, Margarita:** "The Green Snake: An Autobiography" – Floris Books, 2010.

Marie Steiner von Sivers

Participants of the 19-lecture course "Speech and Drama"[1] have formed an ensemble with which Marie Steiner von Sivers cooperated after Rudolf Steiner's death in the following twenty years of her life. If the unique Goetheanum building had not been destroyed by fire on New Year's Eve 1922/23, its stage art had developed in an unimaginable way. Rudolf Steiner had already announced his four mystery dramas for presentation in summer 1923. The actor and eurythmist Edwin Fröböse (1900 - 1997) who belonged to that ensemble expressed in his memoirs on the Festival of St. John in 1978: «The rest of her life, Marie Steiner von Sivers acted loyally towards Rudolf Steiner's intentions and bringing them alive.»[2]

«To start with, Marie Steiner von Sivers directed for the stage of the second Goetheanum the four mystery dramas of Rudolf Steiner. Incessantly she worked on Johann Wolfgang von Goethe's 'Faust' and finally, in 1938, succeeded to put on stage for the first time an unshortened version of his 'Faust I' and 'Faust II'. Besides, she performed plays of Friedrich Schiller, Robert Hamerling, Edouard Schuré and Albert Steffen. She went on numerous tours with an artistic speaking choir which developed from this stage work. In that time, these performances and events under the artistic direction of Marie Steiner von Sivers were in Europe the most famous expression of anthroposophic work. (...) Being Rudolf Steiner's testamentary heiress she also managed the total artistic and literary remains. As she had done already from the beginning, she continued to edit his literary works. This difficult task had been supported by Elisabeth Vreede as of 1918. Of Rudolf Steiner's more than 6,000 free lectures and courses recorded in stenographic transcripts, Marie Steiner von Sivers has edited over 500 more or less comprehensive publications and wrote numerous introductions. (...) These introductions refer to Rudolf Steiner's position in spiritual history under broad world-historical aspects and contain an abundance of common memories. They represent indispensable sources also for the anthroposophic movement's history. To guarantee the continuation of this task, she founded in 1943 – few years before her death – the 'Rudolf Steiner-Nachlassverwaltung' (see Fig. 33).»[3]

---

1 **Steiner, Rudolf:** "Speech and Drama" (CW 282) – Anthroposophic Press Inc; illustr. ed., 1960.
2 **Fröböse, Edwin:** "Mein Weg zur Goetheanum-Bühne" (My Way to the Goetheanum Stage) – Fischer, 1986.
3 Quotations by courtesy of: Stiftung Kulturimpuls, Deutsches Stiftungszentrum, Barkhovenallee 1, 45239 Essen, Germany.

By this act, she created the visible and fertile prerequisites for making accessible to the public the anthroposophic cultural impulse. As of 1961 this association has been editing the volumes of the intended 354 Complete Works of Rudolf Steiner as issues for readers and students – which demands editorial research work from an expert team until today. The result is the perhaps most voluminous edition of a German-speaking author with the most translated works. In 2015, in accordance with a unanimous resolution of the members, the Association was transformed into a Foundation with unchanged purpose: 'Verein zur Verwaltung des literarischen und künstlerischen Nachlasses von Dr. Rudolf Steiner, Dornach' (Foundation to Preserve, Research and Publish Rudolf Steiner's Scientific and Artistic Legacy).

Fig. 33 "Haus Duldeck", accommodating today the "Rudolf Steiner Nachlassverwaltung (Association for Literal and Art Estate of Dr. Rudolf Steiner, Dornach)" – the former residence of the Emil Grosheintz' family.[1]

---

1   Photo Fig. 33: "Haus Duldeck": © Lizenz "Freie Kunst" by Taxiarchos228, 4th August 2011

As of 2002, the foundation is accommodated in the "Duldeck House", which was designed in 1913 for the Grosheintz's family by Rudolf Steiner who commented the building as follows: »It is of importance that such a house could have been built. It stands for a living protest against any traditional building style.«

Marie Steiner von Sivers died on 27th December of 1948 in Beatenberg, Switzerland, just before completion of her 82nd year. Until last, she stayed true to her task she had taken over at the beginning of the 20th century to pave the way for Rudolf Steiner's work into the world.

After Marie Steiner von Sivers' death, Hella Wiesberger (1920 - 2014) took over the edition of Rudolf Steiner's Gesamtausgabe (GA = CW = Complete Works) who, until old age, was the leading personality of the "Rudolf Steiner Archiv" in Dornach.

The German "Marie Steiner Publishing Company" was founded in 2001 by Mr. Otto Ph. Sponsel-Slezak & Mrs. Christa Slezak-Schindler who already guided the "Institut für heilkünstlerische Sprachgestaltung" (Institute for Therapeutic-Artistic Speech Formation). She founded the speech-artistic therapy in the sense of Rudolf Steiner's spiritual science in 1978, was member of the Section of Arts of Eurythmy, Speech, Drama and Music at the Goetheanum until 2005, Member of the Anthroposophical Society until 2009 and participant of the First Class of the School for Spiritual Science. The publishers' target group are people who want to independently practise and develop speech art, connecting anthroposophic meditation and eurythmy to a higher unit of the spoken word.[1]

---

1   "Institut für heilkünstlerische Sprachgestaltung und Marie Steiner Verlag im Haus der Sprache", Burghaldenweg 12/1, 75378 Bad Liebenzell - info@sprachgestaltungskunst.de.

Ita Wegman, M.D.

After Rudolf Steiner's death, Ita Wegman continued to work in her Arlesheim Clinic near Dornach[1] to further develop the anthroposophically enhanced medicine which she had developed with Rudolf Steiner. She also promoted the foundation of therapeutical institutions for children whose soul needed curative education and therapeutic support. In comprehensive letters and numerous journeys she tried to motivate the mostly young physicians «to overcome the existential isolation of the individual physician, standing on his own and being at the same time restricted which can no more be the basis for a future medicine because only the physicians in community could be effective in the healing spirit of Archangel Raphael who is also connected with Archangel Michael in our epoch. If only we as physicians succeed to bear vividly within us all that what Rudolf Steiner has given to us, we will succeed not only to heal ill people but also to spread a healing principle everywhere around us.»[2]

When on 14th April 1935 the managing board of the Anthroposophical Society had suspended Ita Wegman of her activities as Member of the Board and Head of the Section for Medicine of the School for Spiritual Science at the Goetheanum, she retired without defending her tasks or rights (see also Chapter 10). In view of the outer restrictions by the events of war and the Dornach circumstances, her path went inward. In Ascona she found a new abode. Together with the faithful physician Hilma Walter (1893 - 1979) for whom she had sent for, she reconditioned the medical histories of patients she had supervised with Rudolf Steiner.

RECOMMENDATIONS FOR FURTHER LITERATURE
Selg, Peter: "The Last Three Years: Ita Wegman in Ascona 1940 - 1943" – SteinerBooks, 2014.
Walter, Hilma, Rudolf Steiner & Clinical-Therapeutic Institutes in Arlesheim and Ascona (eds.): "Abnormalities in Soul-Spiritual Development: Their Presentation and Possibilities for Treatment: Guidelines to an Understanding of 117 Collected Case Histories with Indications by Rudolf Steiner's Treatment Indications" – Mercury Press, Chestnut Ridge, N.Y., 2011.
id., Norbert Glas & Alexander Leroi (eds.): "Memories of Ita Wegman" – Antroposophical Publishing Co., London 1948.

1   Arlesheim Klinik, Pfeffingerweg 1a, CH-4144 Arlesheim. On 8th June 1921 the "Klinisch-Therapeutisches Institut" was founded in Arlesheim. In 1971 it was renamed in "Ita Wegman Klinik". In 2014 the two neighbour hospitals – "Ita Wegman Klinik" and "Lukas Klinik" – merged together as "Arlesheim Klinik", which celebrated its 100-year anniversary in 2021.
2   Quotations of Ita Wegman in a letter to his colleague Ludwig Engel in 1928.

Fig. 34 "Ita Wegman Archiv", the former residence of Ita Wegman.[1]

Fig. 35 "La Motta" Chapel with fresco of Liane Collot d'Herbois (1907 - 1999).[2]

In 1938, Ita Wegman founded in Switzerland's Brissago "La Motta", a sociotherapeutic residential home for children in need of soul care. Meanwhile this "Sociotherapeutic Institute" is the home of a life community for integrated occupation of adults of both sexes with disabilities.

When Ita Wegman died in 1943 at the age of 67 years on the occasion of a work visit in Arlesheim, her urn was transferred to Brissago and set up in the "La Motta" chapel under a wonderful fresco of the painter and art therapist Liane Collot d'Herbois (1907 - 1999), a close friend of Ita Wegman (see Fig. 35).

Later the ashes of Ita Wegman were buried in a flowerbed outside the chapel. Instead of the urn, nowadays a rock crystal is placed under the fresco.

The "La Motta" chapel today is a place of contemplation and memory not only for the Institute and its community but it is also visited by people from all over the world.

1   The wooden house (see Fig. 34) was built in 1924 and served as home for Ita Wegman until she moved to Ascona in 1940. The house is today in the garden of the "Arlesheim Klinik" and houses the "Ita Wegman Archiv" with Mrs. Wegman's written legacy (e. g. 140 notebooks and some picture material) and the "Ita Wegman Institut".

2   Photo Fig. 35: Fondazione La Motta, Istituto Socioterapeutico (www.la-motta.ch). By courtesy of Riccardo Lüthi, director of the Fondazione, Via Costa di Dentro 5, CH-6614 Brissago.

Margarita Woloschin

In 1917, when Margarita Woloschin had provisionally ended her work at the first Goetheanum, she travelled to Moscow where she intended to stay for a short time. But there the Russian political and social revolution had broken out, a period which abolished the tsar monarchy and adopted a socialist form of government followed by two successive revolutions and a bloody civil war. First, Margarita Woloschin could give courses in painting and Anthroposophy. But finally the daily terror, chaos, battle against hunger, cold and disease made it impossible for Margarita Woloschin to do something senseful.

After five and a half frightful years, she was allowed to leave Russia because of her lung disease. Via the Netherlands and Switzerland she finally arrived in Stuttgart, Germany in 1924, where she stayed until the end of her life.

Margarita Woloschin created almost all altarpieces for the growing communities of religious renewal "Die Christengemeinschaft". She gave painting courses, directed anthroposophic conversation groups and wrote essays. She earned her living by portrait paintings.

Margarita Woloschin understood Rudolf Steiner's far reaching artistic impulse in a way that colours can change themselves and that compositions can be moved to touch spheres of the living.

Her autobiography[1] gives evidence of her phenomenal memory and of the enormous number of people she had met. She died at the age of 91 years.

1   **Woloschin, Margarita:** "The Green Snake: An Autobiography" – Floris Books, 2010.

Albert Steffen

«Not later than as of 1929/30, Albert Steffen's position in the Anthroposophical Society and especially in its managing board was controversial. Different points of view among the members of the board, what already had been noticed in the lifetime of Rudolf Steiner, incompatible temperaments and character traits, but also age differences more and more lead to frictions which increased the problems of cooperation and finally, in the course of the years, made it impossible. (…) In the end, it was Albert Steffen's post-mortal loyalty to Rudolf Steiner that gave him the power, despite all adversities, to carry out his work for the Anthroposophical Society over 40 years in a creative attitude and to thus influence and significantly shape the spiritual orientation of this Society.»[1]

»The 'Haus Hansi' was the quaint and comfortable home of Rudolf Steiner from 1914 to 1924 in the incredibly productive final decade of his life. (…) Marie Steiner von Sivers stayed on in this house for another decade after Rudolf Steiner's death. From 1936 until his death, Albert Steffen, lived in the house with his wife. It accommodates today the 'Albert Steffen Stiftung'(Albert Steffen Foundation) that publishes Steffen's works which otherwise might not find a publisher.»[2]

*Fig. 36   "Albert Steffen Foundation" in Dornach, former "Haus Hansi",
the former domicile of Rudolf Steiner und Marie Steiner von Sivers.*[3]

1   Quotation by courtesy of: Stiftung Kulturimpuls, Deutsches Stiftungszentrum, Barkhovenallee 1, 45239 Essen, Germany.
2   Quotation by courtesy of: John Paull, Ph.D.: "The Home of Rudolf Steiner – Haus Hansi". In: Journal of Biodynamics Tasmania, 2018.
3   Photo Fig. 36: By courtesy of: John Paull, Ph.D. © – Geography & Spatial Sciences, School of Technology, Environments & Design, University of Tasmania – j.paull@utas.edu.au, john.paull@mail.com

Fig. 37   Former residence of Elisabeth Vreede in Arlesheim.[1]

Elisabeth Vreede

«After Rudolf Steiner's death, it was hardly possible for Elisabeth Vreede to express her opinion about the confrontations concerning issues on leadership and organization of the Allgemeine Anthroposophische Gesellschaft AAG (Common Anthroposophical Society). Especially with Marie Steiner von Sivers and Albert Steffen the discussions were unfruitful. After her expulsion by the Society's managing board on Easter 1935 (see also Chapter 10), she was separated from personal contacts as well as from the observatory and the archive, projects which she had built with great dedication and own financial resources. She took refuge in her Dutch home country where she participated in numerous events. Her contacts to England came to an end at the outbreak of World War II. The death of Ita Wegman at the beginning of March 1943, was a great shock for her. Having become ill and in need of care she travelled to Ascona, the last living place of Ita Wegman, and died there after a relapse five month after Ita Wegman on 31st August 1943.

In 1954 was released a book edition of Elisabeth Vreede's publications, available by subscription between September 1927 and August 1930. The Astronomical Letters of Elisabeth Vreede[2] were published with a preface of the English mathematician and physicist George Adams. Despite increasing

---

1   Photo Fig. 37: John Paull, Ph.D. © – (address see Fig. 36, page 95). Dr. John Paull visited Dornach and the Goetheanum with all its surroundings several times taking numerous pictures. Two of them are published in this book with his courtesy. In 1920, Elisabeth Vreede had this house built for herself in Arlesheim near Dornach after a model draft of Edith Maryon and Rudolf Steiner. She lived in it until 1935. Today it is in private use.
2   Vreede, Elisabeth: "Astronomy and Spiritual Science: The Astronomical Letters of Elisabeth Vreede" – SteinerBooks Inc., 2007. »This collection of the astronomical writings by Dr. Elisabeth Vreede is a fascinating compendium of scientific and spiritual knowledge. Between September 1927 and August 1930, Dr. Vreede wrote a monthly "letter," available by subscription, about both modern astronomy and classical astrology in the light of spiritual science. It includes clear explanations of the fundamentals of astronomy and discussions on the role of astrology in the modern world. This collection is also an inspiring presentations of a worldview that sees the stars, planets, and all physical phenomena as manifestations of spiritual beings and spiritual activities.« (Report SteinerBooks Inc, 2007)

resistance of members of the Society's managing board, Elisabeth Vreede often invited him to come to Dornach for lectures and seminars. She also took care of the publication of his basic works on 'Projective Geometry and Mathematics and Physics'.»[1]

Andrej Belyi

In 1929, Andrej Belyj finished his "Reminiscences of Rudolf Steiner"[2] in which he explained his relationship to Rudolf Steiner: «All that I understood and not understood of Rudolf Steiner had the basic theme of a growing blazing enthusiasm, love, confidence, and pleasure that my fate found it worthy to meet him, for he is the most important 'unexpected joy' of my life.»

This book contains reminiscences of Andrej Belyj, Assja Turgenieff and Margarita Woloschin who all knew Rudolf Steiner and saw him frequently. These three Russian people give an especially lively and vivid impression of their personal observations and experiences with Rudolf Steiner.

Andrej Belyj died at the age of 54 years writing the last chapter of his memory trilogy "History of the consciousness soul's formation" dedicated to Anthroposophy.

Lory Maier-Smits

«With Rudolf Steiner's approval, Lory Maier-Smits retired in 1922 slowly from the eurythmy group to totally dedicate to her three children and the social and cultural tasks of her family's industrial companies. After the death of her husband in 1958, a free space for eurythmy arose. When invited, she gave lectures in eurythmy schools, Waldorf schools and anthroposophical branches describing e. g. her very first eurythmy lesson with Rudolf Steiner, and in her 70s she showed gestures, rhythms and leaps of the first eurythmic movements.

In spring 1971 she suffered a stroke, was lovingly cared for by her family and died on 19th September 1971.»[3]

1 Quotation by courtesy of: Stiftung Kulturimpuls, Deutsches Stiftungszentrum, Barkhovenallee 1, 45239 Essen, Germany.
2 **Belyj, Andrej, Assja Turgenieff & Margarita Woloschin:** "Reminiscences of Rudolf Steiner" – Adonis Press, 1987; illustrated by photographs as well as drawings and paintings by Assja Turgenieff and Margarita Woloschin.
3 Quotation by courtesy of: Stiftung Kulturimpuls, Deutsches Stiftungszentrum, Barkhovenallee 1, 45239 Essen, Germany.

Ehrenfried Pfeifer

In his autobiography[1], Ehrenfried Pfeiffer wrote: «Soon after Rudolf Steiner's death each of us had to return to his work and everyday duty, and at once deep human conflicts between the leading personalities of the Society became obvious. In fact, the Society's whole story thereafter was a continuous series of conflicts. These persons of strong personality and determined spirit had to carry on Rudolf Steiner's work as a whole and in many details in the Society, Goetheanum, and Sections.»[2]

Already as a young man, Ehrenfried Pfeiffer became one of the leading representatives whose natural-scientific endeavours were inspired by spiritual sources. Until the end of the 1930s he remained Head of the Research Laboratory at the Goetheanum. During this time he could fully develop his capabilities by lectures and consulting activities at home and abroad, especially at the U.S. "Threefold Farm" in Spring Valley, N.Y.

Around his 28th year, new tasks opened up for Ehrenfried Pfeiffer. The wealthy Dutch Maria Tak van Poortvliet decided to adjust her land in Holland to the biodynamic method. Together with Ehrenfried Pfeiffer and Willem Zeylmans van Emmichoven she founded in 1926 the stock company 'Loverendale', a merger of five farms with an area of about 200 hectares vegetable cultivation, agriculture and pasture. According to Rudolf Steiner's impulse of Social Threefolding, the farms were assigned to "Cultuur-maatschappij Loverendale" Responsible director for the whole enterprise was Ehrenfried Pfeiffer.

Already as of the 1930s, Ehrenfried Pfeiffer cultivated contacts and connections to farmers and land owners in the United States. In the course of time he gave numerous lectures and courses. The publication of his book "Biodynamic Farming and Gardening: Renewal and Preservation of Soil Fertility" (Portal Books 2021) arose further interest in his work, especially in the United States.

In 1939, Ehrenfried Pfeiffer went on extended study trips to the Pyrenees, to Syria, Palestine, Egypt, England, Holland and to the Azores with the aim to visit essential mystery places.

Ehrenfried Pfeiffer lived in Spring Valley and continued his research and lecture activities as of 1948. 14 years later, his forces were exhausted. On 24th November 1961 he suffered a heart attack that caused his death on 30th November. He lived to the age of 62.

---

1   **Pfeiffer, Ehrenfried**: "A Modern Quest for the Spirit (1899 - 1961)" – Mercury Press, 2010.
    By courtesy of: Perseus Publishing House (translation from German 3rd edition), Basel, 2003 (p. 122).
2   Quotations by courtesy of: Stiftung Kulturimpuls, Deutsches Stiftungszentrum, Barkhovenallee 1, 45239 Essen, Germany.

After his death, four lectures of Ehrenfried Pfeiffer's cycle "The Heart as Spiritual Organ of Perception and the Etherization of Blood" were published under the Titel "Heart Lectures" (Mercury Press, Spring Valley 1982 & 1989). The first of these lectures (given on 17ᵗʰ December 1950 in Spring Valley) was printed in German for the first time in his autobiography together with two wonderful colour sketches "Systole" and "Diastole".

In Chestnut Ridge the "Pfeiffer Center"[1] with its "Threefold Educational Foundation" today works with programs and institutions that teach and promote forward-thinking practices in education, agriculture, the arts, spirituality, and social life.

Edmund Pracht und Lothar Gärtner

Edmund Pracht (born 1898 in Berlin, Germany, deceased 1974 in Arlesheim, Switzerland) was elevated in a musical family and learned as a child piano and trumpet. In 1916 he began to study Jura in Berlin, but was called to the arms in 1917. After World War I he studied economics, social sciences and philosophy. In 1921, he made the acquaintance of Rudolf Steiner asking him important questions concerning the future of music. In 1922 he participated with the violin builder Lothar Gärtner[2] (born 1902 in Dresden, Germany, deceased there in 1979) in the pedagogical youth course[3]. In 1923 he broke off his studies and became – together with Lothar Gärtner – member of the guardians' group at the fire ruin of the first Goetheanum.

Both friends listened in Dornach to lectures of Rudolf Steiner, and Edmund Pracht had many opportunities of artistic activities. He accompanied eurythmistic performances on the piano, made studies in painting and sculpture. He occupied intensively with the course of music eurythmy "Eurythmy as Visible Singing" (CW 278) and trained to deepen the musical elements. In his yearning for new sounds, the design emerged to dissolve the components of the piano in leaving only strings and resonator.

---

1   The U.S. "Pfeiffer Center" in 10977 Chestnut Ridge N.Y., 260 Hungry Hollow Road (E-mail: info@pfeiffercenter.org) arose from an anthroposophic community of practical work according to lectures of Rudolf Steiner in 1926. Together with its "Threefold Educational Foundation" (founded in 1965 and located in 140 wooded acres just 30 miles from New York City) it is the basis for the planned project for the development of a biodynamic farm profile in the northern suburbs of New York City.
2   Shop in Germany: W. Lothar Gärtner Atelier für Leierbau GmbH, Fritz-Arnold-Straße 18, 78467 Konstanz, Germany.
3   Steiner, Rudolf: "Youth and the Etheric Heart: Rudolf Steiner Speaks to the Younger Generation" (CW 217) – Anthroposophic Press Inc; illustr. ed., 2007.

According to Edmund Pracht's instructions and drawing, Lothar Gärtner enthusiastically built the first Gärtner lyre in the night from 5th to 6th October in 1926 in its round shape.

The first anthroposophic physician, Ita Wegman, was so fond of the new lyre that she introduced it in the curative education, all the more because this instrument was soon available in different pitches. She asked Edmund Pracht to play this lyre in her curative pedagogic institution "Sun Court" in Arlesheim which exists until today.[1]

In 1938, Lothar Gärtner gained his master's certificate in Konstanz thus introducing the profession of lyre builder as independent handicraft.

In 1955, Edmund Pracht published his "Introduction into the Lyre Play". Though compositionally autodidact, his stream of inspiration which we owe the lyre "as gift from heaven" (cited by a member of the Lyre Association of North America) induced him to create melodies which are sung and played until today. Julius Knierim (1919 - 1999), the German curative educator, musicologist (Ph.D.) and composer, has mainly published vocal and choir compositions and music for lyre. The British composer and lyrist John Billing (born 1952) has published an order-list of his numerous lyre compositions.[2]

All over the world there exist lyrists, lyre associations, lyre orchestras, lyre teachers or lyre courses. And until today – besides e. g. various Gärtner models in Germany – many thousands of lyres have since been built world-wide in round and cornered shapes; uncountable versions have been developed, and still they belong to the original lyre impulse.

The following short compilations shall explain in what way Rudolf Steiner's lectures, books, scripts, letters etc. still have an effect today.

1. «Already in 1884, Rudolf Steiner claimed to liberate the educational system from any state paternalism. The turmoil of World War I caused him to revise this thought in connection with a comprehensive proposal to renew the organization of social life. Emil Molt (commercial advisor, honorary doctorate and director of the Waldorf-Astoria Cigarette Factory) consulted Rudolf Steiner asking him to establish and prepare a school for children of his work-ers and to assume its leadership. His plan was to present a new and sound

---

1 Sonnenhof Arlesheim AG, Obere Gasse 10, 4144 Arlesheim, Switzerland – School Home for chil-dren and young people from four years to grown-up age.
2 **Billing, John:** john_lyre@yahoo.co.uk

education as a gift for the children of the workers and employees of his factory. He had realized that Rudolf Steiner's Anthroposophy provides advice and help for a better education. In the autumn of 1919, the first Free Waldorf School opened up in Stuttgart. It was the starting point for many further school foundations worldwide. In his opening address on 7th September 1919, Rudolf Steiner said among other things: 'May that become vivid education act what we have been able to win by spiritual science. That's what we strive for.' And from autumn 1919 until summer 1924 he lectured on Anthroposophy and educational art in 21 lecture cycles.»[1]

2. One of the first teachers of the Free Waldorf School was Caroline von Heydebrand (1886 - 1938). At the age of 33 years she participated in the school's foundation. In this sphere of action she could develop what she had lived as of her youth and later on had searched for. With her pedagogic masterpiece "Childhood: A Study of the Growing Child"[2] she became the pedagogic source of inspiration for many teachers and pedagogues of following generations.

3. In 2018 there existed worldwide 1,150 Rudolf Steiner-/Waldorf-Schools in 65 countries and 1,817 Waldorf Kindergartens in 67 countries. In 2019 the number of enrollments at Rudolf Steiner Schools or Free Waldorf Schools respectively, amounted to 7,000 pupils for the first time. The number of students of Waldorf pedagogy is increasing, too. (Source: Statistisches Bundesamt, Wiesbaden, Germany – Press Release No. 364, 18. 09. 2019.)

4. From 1903 till 1918, Rudolf Steiner gave public lectures every winter semester in Berlin's Architect House (16 cycles with 230 lectures: CW 52 - CW 67). He explained how questions of life and time arising in a variety of ways can be answered from the anthroposophic point of view. (…) In the words of Marie Steiner von Sivers: «The presentations of Rudolf Steiner have a methodical introduction in spiritual science. For all those people who seek a first encounter with Anthroposophy's content, these recordings are suitable also today.»[3]

---

1   Quotation: Katalog des Gesamtwerks Rudolf Steiner – Rudolf Steiner Verlag, Haus Duldeck, 4143 Dornach, Switzerland. These 21 cycles about Anthroposophy and educational art with almost 200 lecture are published in English (CW 293 - CW 311) by SteinerBooks.
2   **Heydebrand, Caroline:** "Childhood: A Study of the Growing Child" – SteinerBooks, 1988.
3   Quotation: Katalog des Gesamtwerks Rudolf Steiner – Rudolf Steiner Verlag, Haus Duldeck, 4143 Dornach, Switzerland.

5. In 1915, Rudolf Steiner renewed and edited for the stage the Christmas plays that had been collected by Karl Julius Schröer.[1] In Transylvania German immigrants fostered their tradition of performing the "Christmas Plays from Oberufer" (The Paradise Play, The Shepherds Play, and The Kings Play) which are a precious treasure until today. Ever since, many stage performances take place after Rudolf Steiner's directions. In twelve lectures Rudolf Steiner explains how the mysteries of the past are preserved for posterity in sagas, legends or in those folksy plays.[2]

6. At the request of the Imperial Council in Bavaria Count Otto von Lerchenfeld (1868 - 1938) and the Chief of the Emperor's Cabinet Count Arthur Polzer-Hoditz (1869 - 1945) Rudolf Steiner had submitted already in the war year 1917 an extensive memorandum to the essential basic ideas of a threefold order of the social organism, which could have resulted in a political solution for the then stagnating trench warfare. By the lack of decisiveness and courage on behalf of these two personalities it was not realized so that the further war situation run its terrible course. Until today, Rudolf Steiner's threefold order of the social organism is a claim for the concrete transformation of the present federal or centralized system. On the basis of Rudolf Steiners lectures, e.g. "Towards Social Renewal Rethinking the Basis of Society" (CW 23, Rudolf Steiner Press; 4th ed., 2000) the German Institute for Social Threefolding in Berlin (E-Mail: institut@dreigliederung.de) offers courses and seminars in 17 languages.

7. From 1918 till 1924, Rudolf Steiner gave to the audience of eurythmy performances a total of 80 introductions into this new movement art which he had originated.[3] Besides numerous stage performances worldwide, the therapeutical eurythmy which developed from the art eurythmy applies as form of therapy for the anthroposophic medicine until today.

8. «In 1921, some young people contacted Rudolf Steiner to ask his advice for religious acting in the sense of a new spirituality. In their universities they had not found what they were striving for and now encountered

---

1   Schröer, Karl Julius (1825 - 1900) was an Austrian-Hungarian language and literature scientist. He was the mentor of the young student Rudolf Steiner.
2   Steiner, Rudolf: "The Human Spirit Past and Present: Occult Fraternities and the Mystery of Golgatha" (CW 165) – Rudolf Steiner Press, 2016.
3   Steiner, Rudolf: "An Introduction to Eurythmy" (CW 277 - 277a) – Anthroposophic Press Inc, 1983.

Anthroposophy with confidence and hope. After a moment's thought, Rudolf Steiner complied with their requests. He always had put stress on the fact, that the Anthroposophical Society was no church and did not wish to establish a new church. Much more, it leaves freedom to everybody in what way he or she wants to maintain a religious life.» – With these words, Friedrich Rittelmeyer describes in his memoirs[1] the first efforts on the way of a religious renewal movement. In autumn 1921, 40 women and men met for Rudolf Steiner's "Lectures and Courses on Christian-Religious Work"[2] – which prepared the spiritual substance for the foundation of "Die Christengemeinschaft" (The Christian Community) one year later. Until his life's end, Rudolf Steiner accompanied this movement of religious renewal with liturgical texts and advices for the ritual and cult acts. Founded in autumn 1922 in Dornach by a group of 45 theologians, priests, and students of mainly Protestant faith, "Die Christengemeinschaft" exists today in 32 countries with worldwide c. 35,000 members.

9. Besides Ehrenfried Pfeiffer, who emigrated in 1940 to the United States of America to introduce biodynamic agriculture, the Italian Ernesto Genoni (1885 - 1975) became Australia's pioneer of biodynamic agriculture. He met Rudolf Steiner for the first time in 1920 at the Goetheanum. He was there in 1924 when Rudolf Steiner had to retreat to his sickbed in his studio and emigrated to Australia where he became expert for biodynamic agriculture and Anthroposophy. In 1928 he initiated the first Anthroposophy meetings in Melbourne. In 1930 Ernesto made a grand tour of biodynamic enterprises in Europe and met the leading biodynamic advocates and practitioners of the day in Germany, Switzerland and England, including Ehrenfried Pfeiffer. In 1932 he founded the Anthroposophical Society Michael Group in Victoria and became Chairman of the managing board in 1962. The Michael Centre adjoins the Melbourne Rudolf Steiner School and the Melbourne Therapy Centre.[3]

---

1   Rittelmeyer, Friedrich: "Rudolf Steiner Enters My Life" – Literary Licensing, LLC 2013.
2   **Steiner, Rudolf**: (CW 342 - 346): Five volumes with 76 lectures published by Rudolf Steiner Press. E. g.: "The Book of Revelation and the Work of the Priest" (CW 346): 18 lectures & conversations with 57 priests. Dornach Sept. 1924. – Rudolf Steiner Press, 1999.
3   Quotation: Journal of Biodynamics Tasmania, 135/2020 (p. 20 - 23).

Chapter 10

THE ANTHROPOSOPHICAL SOCIETY

A healthy social life is found only when,
in the mirror of each soul,
the whole community finds its reflection,
and when, in the whole community,
the virtue of each one is living.[1]

Rudolf Steiner (1861 - 1925)

On the occasion of the re-foundation of the Anthroposophical Society at the Christmas Conference in Dornach in 1923/24 and based on his extraordinary individuality, Rudolf Steiner had the possibility to lay the basis for the "new mysteries" in direct interaction with St. Michael's current "Zeitgeist". In this way, people who want to unselfishly assume responsibility for Anthroposophy can become more and more concrete to experience the reality of a spiritual world for the practical life.

The formal foundation of the German "Anthroposophische Gesellschaft" took place 2nd/3rd February 1913 in Berlin (following its inauguration on 28th of December 1912 in Cologne). Preceding this event was Rudolf Steiner's separation from the German section of the "Theosophische Gesellschaft" which he had served as general secretary as of October 1902. In a series of lectures collected in eight volumes, Rudolf Steiner spoke about the history of the anthroposophical movement and its Society.[2]

---

1   **Steiner, Rudolf:** "Truth-Wrought-Words: And Other Verses and Prose Passages" (CW 40) – SteinerBooks, 2010. This quote on gratitude was written for Edith Maryon on 5th November 1920.
2   **id.:** (http://www.rudolf-steiner-handbuch.de/images/Handbook.pdf):
     - CW 253 Community Life. Inner Development. Sexuality and the Spiritual Teacher
         (7 lectures and documents, Dornach 1915)
     - CW 254 Occult Movements in the 19th Century (10 lectures, Dornach 1915)
     - CW 255b Anthroposophy and its Defenders
     - CW 257 Awakening to Community (10 lectures, Stuttgart and Dornach 1923)
     - CW 258 The Anthroposophic Movement (8 lectures, Dornach 1923)
     - CW 259 The Year of Destiny 1923 in the History of the Anthroposophical Society –
         From the Burning of the Goetheanum to the Christmas Conference
     - CW 260 The Christmas Conference for the Foundation of the General Anthroposophical Society
         1923-1924
     - CW 260a The Constitution of the General Anthroposophical Society

The sections of Freie Hochschule für Geisteswissenschaft am Goetheanum (School for Spiritual Science at the Goetheanum) are described as follows:

1. Allgemeine Anthroposophie (General Anthoposophy)
2. Jugend (Youth)
3. Naturwissenschaft (Natural Science)
4. Landwirtschaft (Agriculture)
5. Mathematik-Astronomie (Mathematics Astronomy)
6. Redende und musizierende Künste
   (Arts of Eurythmy, Speech, Drama and Music)
7. Bildende Künste (Fine Arts)
8. Schöne Wissenschaften (Literary Arts and Humanities)
9. Pädagogik (Pedagogy)
10. Sozialwissenschaften (Social Sciences)
11. Medizin (Anthroposophical Medicine)

The global society "Allgemeine Anthroposophische Gesellschaft – AAG" (General Anthroposophical Society) is divided in national subsidiaries and these are subdivided in regional, local and factual groups. The statutes of the AAG comply with the legal provisions of a registered association based in Dornach, Switzerland.

Basis of the work still forms the courses of the four volumes of "Esoteric Lessons for the First Class of the School for Spiritual Science at the Goetheanum", which Rudolf Steiner gave to the members of the School in the scope of its "Erste Klassenstunde" (First Class Lesson). However, owing to Rudolf Steiner's illness and subsequent death in March 1925, he was able to make only a beginning by establishing the first of the planned three classes and the various sections.[1] Participants of the Class Lessons should have an appropriate familiarity with the basics of Anthroposophy as well as meditative practice.

A rather discreditable episode of the "Allgemeine Anthroposophische Gesellschaft" occurred in 1935 which was completed in 2018 when members of the Society's general assembly signed a petition to rehabilitate Ita Wegman and Elisabeth Vreede.

The "Initiative zur Rehabilitierung von Ita Wegman und Elisabeth Vreede"[2] published excerpts of an article in "Ein Nachrichtenblatt" (A Bulletin)[3] No. 22 of 30th October 2017 describing the process as follows: «On the basis of a resolution of the General Assembly, Mrs. Ita Wegman, M.D., and Mrs. Elisabeth Vreede, Ph.D., elected as members of the managing

---

1   In a 4-volume-set with 19 lessons, 7 recapitulation lessons; 4 individual lessons given in Dornach, Prague, Berne, and London from February to September 1924, these esoteric lessons are published by Rudolf Steiner Press, 2021 (1,728 pages).
2   "Initiative zur Rehabilitierung von Ita Wegman and Elisabeth Vreede", Dorneckstr. 60, CH-4143 Dornach – info@wegman-vreede.com – http://wegman-vreedecom/wp1/wp-content/uploads/2017/11/Rehabilitierung_Wegman-Vreede_A4.pdf.
3   The online periodical "Ein Nachrichtenblatt" came into being "for friends of Anthroposophy and Members of the Anthroposophical Society" (https:/einnachrichtenblatt.org/). It is located in the Swiss canton Solothurn (Seewen). As of 2011 the engaged editors are Roland Tüscher und Kirsten Juwel.

board by Rudolf Steiner at the Christmas Conference 1923/24, have been dismissed on 14th April 1935. Both were accused of severe offences and destructive behaviour against the Society after Rudolf Steiner's death. These claims were recorded in the so-called "Denkschrift" (Memorandum)[1] which in reality was a pamphlet of 154 pages. This decision had the following consequences: After ten years of activities as members of the Society's managing board, Ita Wegman and Elisabeth Vreede were dismissed and – together with their adepts (numerous highly qualified members of the Society) – excluded from all activities. This caused the separation of whole parts of the movement especially in national Societies of England and the Netherlands.

This resolution was reported in "Nachrichtenblatt der Anthroposophischen Gesellschaft" but never revoked. (…) The reasons indicated in the "Denkschrift" were based on misunderstandings, insinuations and defamations of which some members were aware of already at that time. The full extend of the consequences can hardly be judged.»[2]

In 2018, by the "Initiative to rehabilitate Ita Wegman and Elisabeth Vreede", the injustice against both women was fully rehabilitated at the General Assembly of the General Anthroposophical Society in 2018.

Marie Steiner von Sivers who had participated in the exclusion of her board colleagues Ita Wegman and Elisabeth Vreede, in 1946 also was dismissed from participating in the Society's manager board and organization. By this act, the whole female element of the initial managing board was completely eliminated, though Rudolf Steiner had expressed already in the early esoteric lessons the importance of a balance in male-female effectiveness for the renewed esoteric.

«After Marie Steiner von Sivers' elimination and her death shortly afterwards, the initial managing board had shrunk to a minimum of two members: Albert Steffen – he was 64 at Marie Steiner's death – and Guenther Wachsmuth in his 55th years. It might have been a heavy burden to lead as tandem partners an international society with thousands of members and at the same time the School for Spiritual Science at the Goetheanum. To guarantee the Society's future, Albert Steffen enlarged the managing board at the Society's General Conference in 1949. As new members were added the

---

1   The "Denkschrift" about matters of the "Anthroposophische Gesellschaft" were printed from 1925 till 1935 as manuscript for members of the Society and published by twelve editors.
2   Quotations: https://www.anthroweb.info/geschichte/geschichte-ag/der-prozess-um-den-nachlass-rudolf-steiners.html.

natural scientist Hermann Poppelbaum (1891 - 1979) and the musician Wilhelm Lewerenz (1898 - 1956).»[1]

In 2010 the foundation ELIANT gGmbH[2] – based in Stuttgart, Germany – registered the number of people who have had contact with the anthroposophic movement, i. e. anthroposophs in a broader sense, amounted to more than one million Europeans plus some 100,000 supporters outside Europe. In the strict sense, one can define as an anthroposophist people who are member of the "Allgemeine Anthroposophische Gesellschaft" (AAG). At the turn of the millennium their number amounted to more than 50,000 members, in 2009 to c. 47,000, in 2015 and 2016 c. 45,000 in 35 national societies and 39 groups.[3]

In Germany, according to the "mercurial Publikationsgesellschaft" in Stuttgart, the number of members amounted in 2019 to 12,172 and in 2020 to 11,975.

Information about membership or association work can be obtained at regional centres or local groups or at the Society directly.

In the Society's statutes, paragraph 7 has an extraordinary importance. It says: «The institution of the 'School for Spiritual Science at the Goetheanum' is in the first instance under direct responsibility of Rudolf Steiner, who nominates his co-workers and his possible successor. This paragraph contains everything what is connected with the spiritual function of the leader.» When Rudolf Steiner witnessed his death fully consciously and did not nominate a successor, it was unmistakable that the "Freie Hochschule für Geisteswissenschaft" had no leader anymore, since this task pertains to the "Zeitgeist Michael" himself. (As Archangel Gabriel has been the herald of Christ's bodily-earthly birth, Archangel Michael presents Christ's precursor for the spiritual conception of His entity.) The mystery place of the Goetheanum derives from the spiritual world. The way how St. Michael will decide in the cause has to be accepted as destiny leadership or as spiritual language.

---

1   Quotation: https://www.anthroweb.info/geschichte/geschichte-ag/der-prozess-um-den-nachlass-rudolf-steiners.html.
2   Employees and friends of the European Alliance of Initiatives of Applied Anthroposophy – as of end of March 2019 the non-profit foundation ELIANT – want to contribute to more life quality and cultural diversity in Europe. Its working motto is a postulate of Johann Wolfgang von Goethe: "A single person does not help, but he who unites with many at the right hour." – https://eliant.eu/ueber-uns/
3   These data originate from various editions of "Mitteilungen aus der anthroposophischen Arbeit in Deutschland", a component of the periodical "Anthroposophie weltweit". It appears five times a year and is distributed free to all members of the "Anthroposophical Society in Germany". At Easter, St. Johann, Michaelmas and Christmas they are dispatched together with the quarterly journal "Anthroposophie". Every year in June, a separately dispatched special issue goes to the members to invite them for the annual meeting of the Society.

CONCLUSION

Anthroposophy is a path of knowledge,
to guide the spiritual in the human being
to the spiritual in the universe.[1]

Rudolf Steiner (1861 - 1925)

The following text derives from a speech Rudolf Steiner held in Vienna to the members of the Anthroposophical Society on 14th April 1914 within the scope of his six-lecture cycle "The Inner Nature of Man – And our Life between Death and Rebirth."[2]

«Before I come today to the lecture itself, I wish to address some words to you only saying that we will have the next similar meeting not in midsummer time as we did the last years in Munich but hopefully in the last two months of this year, because it shall take place already in the Goetheanum building[3]. Unfortunately, the finalization of this building takes longer than originally planned. But then we should be able to open the Goetheanum with a festive event.

This building causes us more work than one can usually imagine and, therefore, you will understand that for a certain time the personal conversations cannot take place already now.

For our Austrian friends it has surely not been easy to familiarize with the idea that the Goetheanum will now be in such a far distance. Yet, despite I have not enough time for the moment to give more explanations, the circumstances have led our karma to erect the Goetheanum at the Dornach hill, and that will be good.

It will have to be before our eyes that we regard this building as a kind of central site and symbol of our spiritual movement.»

---

1   **Steiner, Rudolf** in: "Anthroposophical Leading Thoughts: Anthroposophy as a Path of Knowledge: The Michael Mystery" (CW 26) – Rudolf Steiner Press; 3rd ed., 1999. – Translation of the quote by George and Mary Adams. This key volume – written from 1923 - 1925 for the members of the General Anthroposophical Society– contains in brief paragraphs Rudolf Steiner's spiritual science, Anthroposophy, as a modern path of knowledge. Invaluable as clear summaries of Rudolf Steiner's fundamental lines of thought, they are intended not as doctrine, but as a stimulus and focus for study and discussion. Their intention, as Rudolf Steiner states, is to contribute to a «unity and organic wholeness of the work of the Society without there being any question of constraint».
2   **id.:** "The Inner Nature of Man: And our Life between Death and Rebirth." (CW 153) – Rudolf Steiner Press; rev. ed. 2013.
3   In this speech, Rudolf Steiner still speaks of "Johannes Building". To avoid unnecessary irritation, I used the later introduced denomination "Goetheanum Building".